Ex Líbrís

GETTYSBURG
A BATTLEFIELD ATLAS

GETTYSBURG
A BATTLEFIELD ATLAS

by Craig L. Symonds

Cartography by William J. Clipson

The Nautical & Aviation Publishing Company of America
Baltimore, Maryland

Library of Congress Catalog Card Number : 91-40093

ISBN : 1-877853-16-X

Printed in the United States of America
Second printing, Aug 1992

Library of Congress Cataloging in Publication Data

Symonds, Craig L.
Gettysburg, a battlefield atlas
by Craig L. Symonds; cartography by William J. Clipson.
ISBN 1-877853-16-X
1. Gettysburg (Pa.), Battle of, 1863—Maps.   I. Clipson, William J.
II. Title.
G1264.G3S5S8 1992 (G&M)
973.7'349'0223—dc20
91-40093   CIP   MAP

Jacket Photograph: Courtesy of The National Park Service, Gettysburg National Military Park / Eisenhower National Historic Site.

Frontis Photograph: Courtesy of Gettysburg National Military Park.

To Those Who Fought

". . . we cannot dedicate, we cannot consecrate, we cannot hallow this ground. The brave men living and dead who struggled here have consecrated it far above our poor power to add or detract."

—Abraham Lincoln

CONTENTS

KEY TO MAP SYMBOLS

 Infantry units (see explanation at right)

 Former position of infantry units

 Cavalry units

 Artillery (depicts location, not precise number of guns)

 Route of march

 Army headquarters

 Attack

 Site of skirmish

 Woods

Swamp

Stone wall

Railroad

INTRODUCTION

Gettysburg was the greatest battle in the history of the Western Hemisphere. A great deal has been written about it, and this slim volume makes no pretense to breaking new ground nor to being in any way definitive. It is designed to provide a cartographic and narrative overview of the Gettysburg campaign. It can serve as an introduction for a the novice, as a guide for a visitor to the battlefield, and for the interested student at every level.

The map symbols shown at left are largely self-explanatory, but one point needs to be made about the depiction of infantry units. Since the goal of this volume is clarity rather than exhaustive detail, it is important to note that the boxes depicted on the maps to show the location of military units do not in every case conform to the precise number of military units at that location, but instead portray the location and relative strength of the forces present. This was necessary because Federal and Confederate corps and divisions were not comparably sized. A Federal corps might number between eight and twelve thousand, while a Confederate corps could be twice as large. In order to ensure that the proportional strength of each side was perceptible at a glance, those maps where the movements of whole army corps are portrayed (Maps 1-5 and Map 23), show two blocks to indicate the location of a Confederate corps, but only one to show the location of a Federal corps. Since in this campaign the Confederates had three corps and the Federals seven, the overall proportional strength is fairly depicted.

On most of the rest of the maps, each block indicates the location of a brigade—Union or Confederate, though on three of the maps, a key in the corner indicates that each box represents a regiment. Though it is difficult to attach specific troop strengths to these units, the scale below is a rough guide:

Union		Confederate
8,000 - 12,000	CORPS	16,000 - 22,000
3,000 - 5,000	DIVISIONS	4,000 - 8,000
1,000 - 2,500	BRIGADES	1,500 - 3,000
200 - 800	REGIMENTS	200 - 500

In theory, each corps contained three divisions, each division three brigades, and each brigade three to five regiments. The extent to which actual unit organizations reflected this ideal is evident from a glance at the order of battle for both armies which is provided as Appendix A on page 91.

The text accompanying each map is necessarily brief, but as in my previous battlefield atlases, I have taken the liberty of going beyond a strict narrative description to provide sketches of the principal commanders, and also to offer conclusions of my own about the more controversial aspects of the campaign.

I am once again indebted to Bill Clipson for his faithful rendering of the twenty–four maps in the book. Bill is a perfectionist, and any error that may exist on any map is due solely to me rather than to him. I also want to thank my colleague at the Naval Academy, Dr. Nancy Ellenberger, for allowing me to include an excerpt from a letter written by her great–great–grandfather, Captain Samuel Trouant Keene of the 20th Maine.

Craig L. Symonds
Annapolis, Maryland

PROLOGUE
The Civil War
at Flood Tide

It was nine o'clock and full dark when the shell hit. Major General Joseph ("Fighting Joe") Hooker was leaning against a wooden column on the veranda of the Chancellor mansion, which the overworked Union doctors had turned into a field hospital, when a solid shot from an unseen Confederate artillery piece smashed into the column and shattered it. Hooker was thrown violently to the porch floor and lay there stunned. Ever since dusk the Confederates had been pressing the Union right flank, trying to drive Hooker's army away from the roads that led back over the Rappahannock which his men had crossed so confidently only days before. Now enemy shells were landing about his own headquarters, and this one had nearly killed him. His staff helped him to his feet; though he was groggy, he did not appear to be seriously hurt. His aides carried him out to the yard and laid him down on a blanket. Fortified by a shot of brandy, he rose tentatively to his feet and called for his horse; this was no time for a commanding general to be lying down. Moving slowly, possibly in shock, Hooker mounted his horse and prepared to ride off. At that moment the blanket where he had been lying was struck by another Confederate shell

"Stonewall" Jackson returns to the Confederate lines after his reconnaissance of the Federal position at Chancellorsville on the evening of May 2. Within moments a volley from his own troops would hurl him from his saddle mortally wounded. (Battles and Leaders of the Civil War)

which virtually disintegrated it. Hooker turned his horse toward the rear and, surrounded by his staff, headed northward.

It had all started so promisingly. Planned in secret for much of the spring, Hooker had set his grand offensive in motion a week before, sending his cavalry on a raid into the rebel rear to distract J.E.B. Stuart and the Confederate cavalry. Thus protected, he hoped, from the prying eyes of the gray troopers, he sent three full infantry corps on a long roundabout march to the fords over the Rappahannock twenty miles upstream from his position across from the rebel stronghold at Fredericksburg. Successfully gaining the southern bank, he had then settled down to wait for Lee to react. Surely the old fox would have no option now but to retreat. He had been outflanked, and he was hugely outnumbered—nearly two to one. Hooker had Lee just where he wanted him.

The first evidence that Hooker had seriously miscalculated came at dusk on May 2 when 25,000 Confederates smashed into his unprotected right wing. Acting on Lee's orders, Stonewall Jackson had executed a dramatic day-long march around Hooker's entire army to fall on the Federal corps of Major General Oliver Otis Howard. Completely surprised, Howard's corps broke apart almost at once. Hooker reacted swiftly, sending in his reserves to bolster the disintegrating line. But the rebels continued to advance, and even after dark they pressed forward. Now as Hooker rode rearward, stunned by his brush with a horrible

Joseph ("Fighting Joe") Hooker was stunned, both figuratively and literally, by the Confederate onslaught in the wilderness around the Chancellor House. Though sustained by Lincoln after his defeat, his subsequent squabbling with the administration during the early phases of the Gettysburg campaign would cost him his job. (Library of Congress)

death, he abandoned all thought of his grand offensive. His mind turned instead to escape. Collapsing onto a cot in his headquarters tent, he ordered his subordinates to pull the army back into a defensive position around the fords over the river.

At almost the same moment that Hooker fell to the porch floor, about a mile to the west Stonewall Jackson was being lowered to the ground, wounded in his arm and side. All evening he had driven his men forward like one possessed. "Press them!" he cried during the assault. "Cut them off. . . . Press them!" Not satisfied with routing the foe, Jackson wanted to destroy his enemies—to smite them hip and thigh and purge them from Virginia. He pushed ahead past his soldiers and personally reconnoitered the darkened roads which he hoped would provide him the means to intercept the Federal retreat. He was returning to his own lines around nine o'clock—a shadowy mounted figure in the woods—when a ragged volley rang out from the butternut clad veter-

ans. "Cease firing! Cease firing!" Jackson's escort shouted. "You are firing into your own men!" Not all could hear him; many who did hear refused to believe it. They fired another volley. When the firing died out, the truth was learned. Jackson was hit—hit three times, and by his own men. He did not seem to be badly hurt, his greatest disappointment at the moment was that he could not press ahead with the attack he had planned. No one knew yet that his arm would require amputation, or that pneumonia would set in, or that eight days later he would be dead.

The Battle of Chancellorsville was perhaps the greatest Confederate victory of the American Civil War. Outnumbered two to one, and caught between the pincers of a cleverly-devised strategic maneuver, Lee responded with breathtaking audacity, dividing his forces twice and thus seizing the initiative. His gamble had been rewarded with victory, but it had come at a terrible cost. Some 13,000 Southern soldiers fell during the two day fight, and one of them was Stonewall Jackson who would be irreplacable. And though Northern losses were even greater (some 17,000), Confederate losses constituted 21 percent of those engaged while Federal losses constituted only 14 percent. Many more such victories would doom the Southern cause. Still, a victory was a victory. Once again Lee's army had demonstrated that the Yankees crossed the Rappahannock only at their peril.

The South's celebration of this victory was muted not only by the news of Jackson's wound and subsequent death, but also by the war news from elsewhere in the Confederacy. In Mississippi, the stoic and phlegmatic Ulysses S. Grant, after floundering around in the swamps west of Vicksburg for half a year, had finally found a way to bring his superior forces to bear against the "Gibraltar of the West." On the day of the Battle of Chancellorsville, his men brushed aside a defending Confederate force at Port Gibson, thirty miles south of Vicksburg, and proceeded to march inland toward Jackson, the Mississippi state capital, which fell on May 14. The defenders of Vicksburg, some 30,000 men under John C. Pemberton, were thus cut off from the rest of the Confederacy and doomed to withstand a siege unless reinforcements could be sent from elsewhere in the Confederacy to succor them.

The Confederate President, Jefferson Davis, was particularly concerned about the threat in Mississippi. He was himself a Mississippian, and his home—Brierfield Plantation—was only fifteen miles south of Vicksburg. Moreover, the fall of that city would give the Yankees control of the Mississippi and effectively divide the Confederacy in half. With Pemberton under siege at Vicksburg, did it not follow that all efforts should be made to hold that citadel? James Longstreet's corps had missed the fight at Chancellorsville, having spent the month of May in the vicinity of Suffolk. Now Davis proposed that in light of the victory at Chancellorsville, Longstreet and his men might be sent westward to Mississippi. Lee could fall back on Richmond and stand on the

Oliver Otis Howard was the unlucky commander of the Federal Eleventh Corps. The rout of his corps at Chancellorsville not only undermined the confidence of the high command in Howard, but perhaps, too, it undermined his soldiers' confidence in themselves. (Library of Congress)

Thomas J. "Stonewall" Jackson was Lee's strong right arm until his death a few days after the Battle of Chancellorsville. He was an eccentric personality, often-brilliant, though sometimes-erratic. After his death, however, he was deified by the Southern population. (Library of Congress)

defensive until the situation in Mississippi was resolved. Davis asked Lee to come to Richmond to discuss it. Lee stayed three days in Richmond, May 14–17. Arguably, they were the three most decisive days of the war, for they doomed Pemberton and Vicksburg to defeat, and set Lee's magnificent army on the road to Gettysburg.

As always Lee listened respectfully to Davis's proposal, but he argued that the key to military success was not in the West. The war would be won or lost, he said, in the East. Perhaps he was fated to this conclusion. Lee's commitment to the Southern cause did not really extend beyond the boundaries of his beloved Virginia. After all, if his native state had remained with the Union, Lee might conceiv-

Robert E. Lee was a daring tactician who surprised Hooker at Chancellorsville by twice dividing his army. After his stunning victory, he argued against sending troops from Virginia to Mississippi, and urged instead that the Army of Northern Virginia move north into Pennsylvania to take the war to the enemy. (Library of Congress)

ably have found himself commanding the army in blue rather than the one in gray. Now the thought of sending troops from Virginia to Mississippi struck him as a very bad idea. He argued an alternative proposal: that his army should take the offensive, carry the war from Virginia into Pennsylvania, and there deliver the blow that would convince the administration in Washington to end its effort to hold the Southern states in the Union by force. His army had never been stronger; morale had never been higher; Hooker was still reeling from his setback at Chancellorsville. This was the time to strike north and seek the decisive confrontation. Davis agreed. Vicksburg would have to look out for itself; Lee's army was going north.

THE ARMIES MOVE NORTH
May–June, 1863

With the death of "Stonewall" Jackson on May 10, Lee lost his strong right arm. The stately Lee and the enigmatic Jackson had worked so well together that it seemed to some their minds worked in tandem. "I have but to show him my design," Lee once said of Jackson, "and I know that if it can be done it will be done. No need for me to send or watch him. Straight as the needle to the pole he advances to the execution of my purpose." Now Jackson was gone beyond recovering. Some historians have speculated that had Jackson lived, the South might have won the war—such is his historic reputation. Without a doubt Jackson's loss was a very real blow to the South, if for no other reason than because the South believed it to be so. But at least part of Jackson's mythic place in history derives from his timely departure from life; nothing so ensures immortality as a dramatic death at the moment of victory.

Whatever might or might not have happened had Stonewall lived, Lee now had to plan his forthcoming campaign without him. The old command structure, in which Jackson

Confederate infantry crosses the Potomac River into Maryland near Williamsport as the Army of Northern Virginia begins its second "invasion" of the North. (Library of Congress)

and Longstreet had each commanded a wing of the army, now struck Lee as too unwieldy for an army grown to over 70,000 men. Lee decided to reorganize the army into three corps. Longstreet, the massive and brooding old War Horse, would retain command of the First Corps. Lee chose Richard S. (Dick) Ewell, the bald-headed little general whose large eyes and beak-like nose reminded so many of a pecking bird, to assume the mantle of the Second Corps, and Lee took one division from each of these existing corps to create a third. Command of this new corps would fall on Ambrose Powell (A. P.) Hill. Like Ewell, "Little Powell" was small of stature so that Longstreet towered over both of his fellow corps commanders in both experience and physical mass. Neither Ewell nor Hill had ever led a corps into battle, but Lee was confident of their ability to do so. He wrote to Davis that Ewell was "an honest, brave soldier, who has always done his duty well," and that Hill was "the best soldier of his grade with me." If neither man was Jackson, there was nevertheless experience, skill, and determination there.

A few knowledgeable observers had speculated that Lee might give Jackson's old corps to the man who had commanded it in the closing hours of the Battle of Chancellorsville: James Ewell Brown Stuart, known to all as "Jeb." Just turned thirty, Stuart was young for a corps

Richard S. Ewell did not look like a hero with his bald head and prominent beak, but his war record and reliability convinced Lee to choose him to lead the Second Corps, Jackson's old command. His detractors would later claim that he was certainly no Jackson, and some would argue that he lost an irretrievable opportunity to finish off the Union army during the first day's fight at Gettysburg. (Library of Congress)

command, but he was popular with the men and had proven himself in all the campaigns from Manassas to Chancellorsville. Lee, too, enjoyed the companionship of his irrepressible cavalry commander, and relied upon him for intelligence of the enemy's movements. Stuart may have been disappointed not to receive a corps command, but his importance to the army was recognized by a promotion to lieutenant general and confirmation of his role as the commander of what amounted to a grand division of cavalry.

Thus the new organization of the Army of Northern Virginia looked like this:

First Corps — James Longstreet
Second Corps — Richard Ewell
Third Corps — A. P. Hill
Cavalry Division — J. E. B. Stuart

The Army of Northern Virginia was a tempered and dangerous instrument of war ready to do its commander's bidding.*

North of the Rappahannock, Hooker, too, had to re-evaluate his strategy and his army in light of the Battle of Chancellorsville. Unchastened by his defeat, Hooker soon reverted to the confident, even cocky, commander who had assured President Lincoln five months ago that he could end the rebellion. He had ascended to the command of the Army of the Potomac only in January, replacing the unlucky Ambrose Burnside who reverted to a corps command. Hooker had been critical of Burnside's leadership, and his self assurance

_____
*For a more complete order of battle, see Appendix A.

Ambrose Powell Hill was elevated to the rank of lieutenant general and entrusted with command of the newly-created Third Corps. His corps was the second in line behind Ewell's on the long march into Pennsylvania, but his would be the first troops to fight at Gettysburg. (Library of Congress)

and his well-advertised political views had endeared him to the Radical element in Lincoln's cabinet. Secretary of the Treasury Salmon P. Chase in particular argued that Hooker would bring more assertiveness to army command. There was little else in Hooker's war record to recommend him. His nickname, which implied aggressive instincts, was actually the result of a punctuation error in an 1862 telegram. In a terse wire meant to note only that Hooker's division was engaged with the enemy, "Fighting—Joe Hooker" was transcribed as "Fighting Joe Hooker," and Fighting Joe he was ever after.

Hooker parceled out blame for his defeat at Chancellorsville to George Stoneman, his cavalry commander, who had failed to distract Stuart; to Oliver O. Howard, whose German-speaking troops had borne the brunt of Jackson's assault; and to various others. Of his own role in the battle, all he would admit was that for a brief moment he had lost confidence

in himself. It was a most charitable view of events. After a good start, he had lost his nerve and surrendered the initiative to Lee. Given the history of revolving commanders in the Army of the Potomac (there had already been three changes of command), Hooker had reason to fear that he might be the next to go.

For his part, Lincoln had never possessed unalloyed confidence in Hooker's ability. Only with reluctance had he allowed Chase and others to convince him that Hooker should be given his chance. Through the first months of the new year, the increased morale in the army had fed Lincoln's hope that his initial skepticism had been misplaced. Now it all came back in a rush. His disappointment was shared by some in the army. When Lincoln visited the army five days after the battle, Darius N. Couch, commander of the Second Corps, told the president that he would no longer serve under Hooker, and urged him to appoint George Gordon Meade, commander

James E. B. Stuart remained in command of an expanded Confederate cavalry division after the reorganization in May. His splendid war record was blemished soon afterward by the embarrassment of the skrimish at Brandy Station (see MAP #2), but his greatest error was conducting a prolonged raid around the Union army when his primary responsibility was screening the Confederate infantry. (Library of Congress)

of the Fifth Corps, to replace him. At least two other corps commanders concurred with Couch's recommendation. But Lincoln was reluctant to change commanders again—there had been too much of that already. For now, the president was satisfied to encourage Hooker to put the army in order and suggest that he should not be in a hurry to renew the campaign. True to his word, Couch quit the army in disgust and was replaced by the as-yet unproven Winfield S. Hancock. Hooker retained his command, but he had the sense to perceive that he was on probation.

Organizationally, the Army of the Potomac was divided into seven infantry corps, each numbering between nine and thirteen thousand men, about half the size of a Confederate corps.*

First Corps — John F. Reynolds
Second Corps — Winfield S. Hancock
Third Corps — Daniel E. Sickles
Fifth Corps — George Gordon Meade
Sixth Corps — John Sedgwick
Eleventh Corps — Oliver Otis Howard
Twelfth Corps — Henry W. Slocum
Cavalry Division — Alfred Pleasonton

*For a more complete order of battle, see Appendix A.

The commanders of these seven corps were a mixed lot. Some, like Reynolds and Meade, were proven combat veterans. Others, like Sickles and Slocum, had acquired their positions largely due to their political influence and had yet to demonstrate any real gift of command. Still others, like Hancock and Pleasanton, had promise but little experience. Howard, who was a competent soldier, was still scarred by the memory of that awful night at Chancellorsville when his corps broke and fled. Then, too, perhaps some of the corps commanders wondered about Hooker. How had Chancellorsville affected him? Though superior in numbers, the Army of the Potomac was short on self confidence. The men in the ranks were as willing as ever, but they had developed a kind of fatalism about themselves and their army. If, as Napoleon had claimed, the moral was to the physical as three is to one, the Army of the Potomac was outnumbered indeed.

James Longstreet was Lee's most experienced corps commander. Physically large, dark, and brooding, he was also cautious. His reluctance to accept the necessity of assuming the tactical offensive at Gettysburg led him into conflict with his commander, and is the centerpeiece of the most controversial aspect of the Gettysburg campaign. (Cook Collection, Valentine Museum)

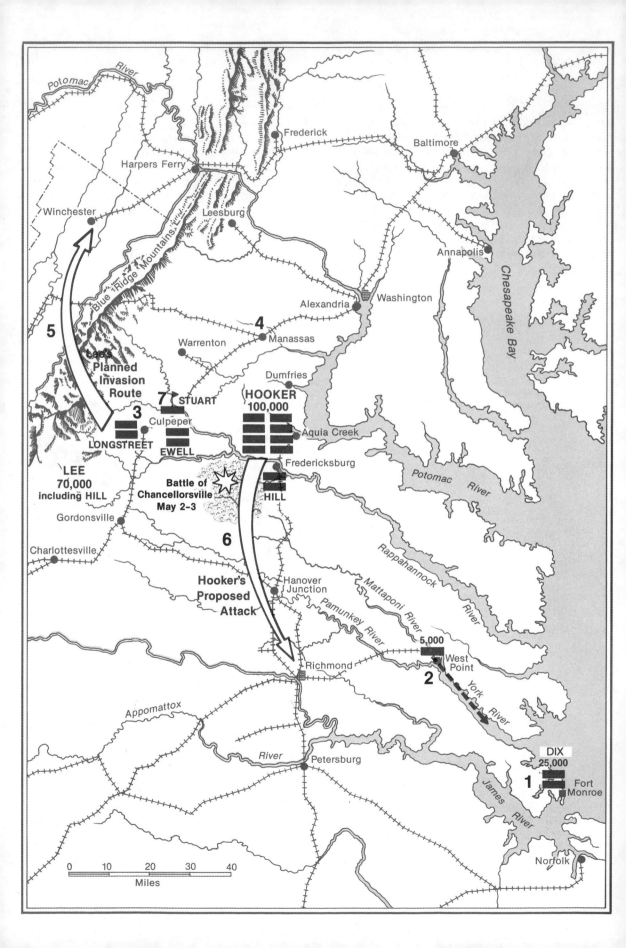

Potomac River

Frederick

Baltimore

Harpers Ferry

Winchester

Leesburg

Annapolis

Chesapeake Bay

5

Lee's Planned Invasion Route

Blue Ridge Mountains

Alexandria

Washington

4

Warrenton

Manassas

Dumfries

7 STUART

HOOKER
100,000

3
LONGSTREET

Culpeper

Aquia Creek

EWELL

Fredericksburg

LEE
70,000
including HILL

Battle of
Chancellorsville
May 2–3

HILL

Potomac River

Gordonsville

6

Charlottesville

Hooker's
Proposed
Attack

Hanover
Junction

Rappahannock River

Mattaponi River

Pamunkey River

5,000

West
Point

2

York River

Richmond

Appomattox

River

Petersburg

James River

DIX
25,000

1

Fort
Monroe

0   10   20   30   40
Miles

Norfolk

MAP 1

Lee Takes the Offensive

June 3–8, 1863

Lee's plan for a grand invasion of the North was complicated by the fact that substantial Union forces still held a toe-hold on the Virginia peninsula formed by the York and James Rivers (1). It was there that Lee had won his first great victories in the summer of 1862, driving the army of Union commander George B. McClellan away from the gates of Richmond. But the Federals had not abandoned the peninsula. Major General John A. Dix commanded upward of 30,000 men in the vicinity of Fort Monroe, including an outpost of 5,000 at West Point on the York River, only 35 miles from Richmond (2). If Lee took the Army of Northern Virginia northward, would Dix be tempted to pounce on Richmond? Such a "pounce" would be uncharacteristic of the Federals, especially after Chancellorsville, but Lee was nonetheless gratified to learn on June 2 that the 5,000 men at West Point were pulling out and returning to Fort Monroe. The move left him free to begin his grand offensive.

It began in the pre-dawn darkness of June 3. Two divisions of Longstreet's corps—those of Major Generals John B. Hood and Lafayette McLaws—which had been guarding the fords across the Rappahannock west of Fredericksburg, pulled back and headed westward toward Culpeper, some 30 miles away (3). They were followed by the divisions of Ewell's Second Corps. Hill's newly-formed Third Corps remained behind at Fredericksburg to guard against a Federal push across the river. That same night, Lee himself headed west, establishing his headquarters at Culpeper Court House.

Hooker suspected that Lee planned to move his army northeastward along the line of the Orange & Alexandria Railroad toward Manassas Junction (4) to seek yet a third Confederate victory on that bloody ground. But Lee had even grander plans: he would march his army even further west, through the passes in the Blue Ridge, and north through the lush Shenandoah Valley (5). There the rich farm land could supply his army, and the Blue Ridge itself would screen his movements from Federal cavalry patrols. The Blue Ridge (and South Mountain, its extension into Maryland) marched northward

for a hundred miles. Hooker would never know when or where Lee might return through one of the many gaps in that granite fence to offer battle.

If Hooker underestimated the ambition of Lee's movement, he had little doubt about how to respond to it. On June 5, he wrote to Lincoln to report that the Army of Northern Virginia was preparing to move northward again, perhaps on another invasion into Maryland. After explaining the situation, he proposed that his own army launch a full-scale attack on Hill's lone corps at Fredericksburg. The Army of the Potomac would surely overwhelm such a paltry force, or alternatively, it would force Lee to rush back to Fredericksburg to prevent Hill from being destroyed. If Lee did not return to help Hill, Hooker could follow up his easy victory with a move southward to capture Richmond which would be virtually undefended (6).

Lincoln did not like the idea. From the beginning, Lincoln and Halleck had impressed upon Hooker the necessity of keeping the Army of the Potomac between Lee's main body and Washington. The president was not willing to let Hooker get himself involved in another full scale battle south of the Rappahannock while Lee with over 50,000 men marched into Pennsylvania. "In case you find Lee coming to the North of the Rappahannock," Lincoln wired back, "I would by no means cross to the South of it." Lincoln noted that Hill would almost certainly fight from entrenchments which would give him a tactical advantage. Hooker's anticipated easy victory might not be so easy after all. While Hooker sought to drive Hill from Fredericksburg, Lee might very well come up behind Hooker, cutting the Federal army off from Washington, and pinning it between two enemy forces. Lee's hammer might smash Hooker against Hill's anvil. In characteristically colorful language, Lincoln suggested that the Army of the Potomac might find itself caught athwart the Rappahannock "like an ox jumped half over a fence and liable to be torn by dogs front and rear, without a fair chance to gore one way or kick the other."

The Federal Chief of Staff, Henry Wager Halleck, followed up the president's cautionary advice with a telegram of his own. "Would it not be more advantageous to fight his [Lee's] movable column first?" he asked. In other words, rather than attack the tail of the rebel column, Hooker should seek to engage its head, and above all, he should keep his own army between Lee and Washington. First, however, he might have a chance to strike at the Confederate force gathering at Culpeper, or Jeb Stuart's cavalry division at Brandy Station (7). For this purpose, Hooker summoned his cavalry commander to his headquarters.

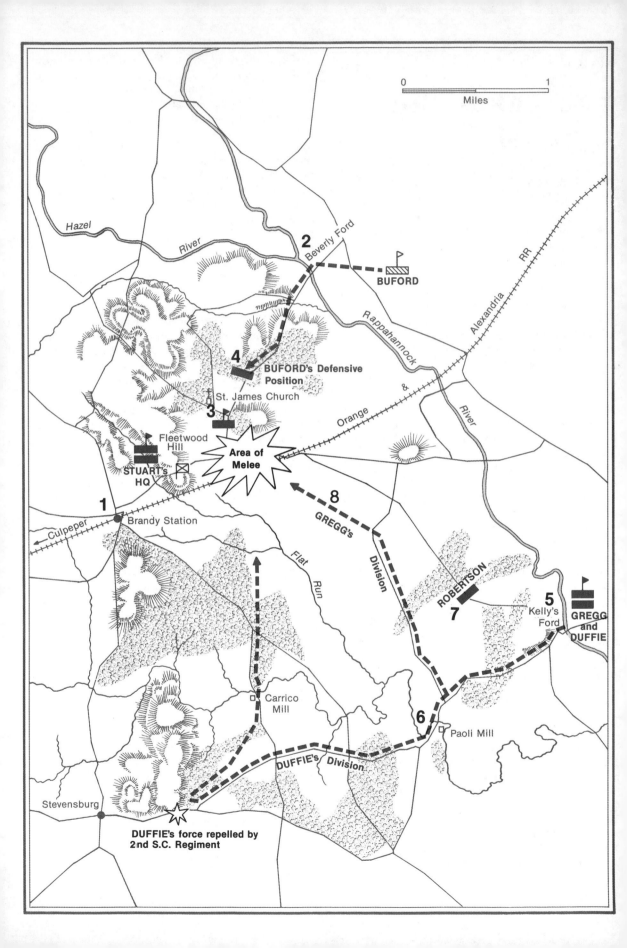

0   1
Miles

Hazel

River

Beverly Ford

2

BUFORD

Rappahannock

Alexandria

RR

4

BUFORD's Defensive Position

† St. James Church

3

Orange

&

River

Fleetwood Hill

STUART's HQ

Area of Melee

8

GREGG's

1

Culpeper

Brandy Station

Flat

Run

Division

ROBERTSON

7

Kelly's Ford

5

GREGG and DUFFIE

Carrico Mill

6

Paoli Mill

DUFFIE's Division

Stevensburg

DUFFIE's force repelled by 2nd S.C. Regiment

MAP 2

Brandy Station

June 9, 1863

While the Confederate infantry tramped westward, Jeb Stuart concentrated his cavalry in the rolling countryside north of Culpeper around Brandy Station (1). There, on June 7, he held a grand review of his enlarged command. The ranks of assembled troopers stretched for more than a mile across the open terrain; three bands played martial airs as ten thousand mounted men passed in review. Then the cavalry brigades engaged in a mock battle, charging the horse artillery which fired blank cartridges. The men cheered, the ladies applauded, the general smiled. It was a splendid show. That night, the officers attended a ball in their honor. Stuart's mind was easy. He did not believe he had anything to fear from the Federal cavalry; like most southern cavalrymen, he was all but dismissive of the fighting ability of the blue-coated cavalry. It was a disdain he would soon have an opportunity to rue.

Stuart's Federal counterpart was handsome, dark-eyed Major General Alfred Pleasanton who had replaced the discredited George Stoneman in late May. Even before Stuart staged his grand review, Hooker ordered Pleasanton to take three divisions of cavalry (about 8,000 men), plus 3,000 infantry, to Culpeper to destroy whatever enemy force he found there. Pleasanton left the next day (June 8) with six brigades of cavalry and one of infantry to teach Stuart a lesson in humility.

Pleasanton divided his command into two wings, one under John Buford, and another under David McM. Gregg. Crossing the Rappahannock at widely separated fords, they would close on Stuart's encampment at Brandy Station and catch the enemy in a classic pincer movement.

In a dense fog, Buford's men splashed across Beverly Ford (2) just before dawn on June 9. His troopers drove off the rebel pickets and advanced quickly against disorganized opposition toward Fleetwood Hill, the dominating geographical feature in the area, and the site of Stuart's headquarters. About two miles south of the river near St. James Church (3), they encountered about 150 men of the 7th Virginia cavalry, some of them still in their night-clothes, who fiercely contested the Federal advance. Other rebel forces, drawn to the firing, soon joined them, and by mid-morning, the Confederates had assembled sufficient force to launch a counterattack. Stuart himself dashed to the scene of the fight from his command tent atop Fleetwood Hill. Outnumbered now, Buford withdrew to the treeline north of St. James Church and went over to the defensive (4).

So far, Buford's single division had borne the brunt of the day's fighting, for Gregg's two divisions got a late start and not until seven o'clock did they cross the river at Kelley's Ford, six miles downstream (5). Gregg's orders were to take one division northward to join Buford near Brandy Station and send the other (Alfred N. Duffie's) westward toward Stevensburg. But instead, Gregg took both divisions toward the southwest and did not turn north until he reached Paoli Mill (6). Though accidental, Gregg's detour proved to be fortuitous, for Stuart had anticipated an attack from Kelly's Ford, and had sent the 1,500-man brigade of Beverly Robertson to block the direct route northward (7). Gregg's detour allowed him to by-pass these troops, and thus it was that while Buford was being gradually forced back in the fighting around St. James Church, the Confederates who were left atop Fleetwood Hill were astonished to see Gregg's men advancing toward them from the southwest (8). The only Confederate force on Fleetwood Hill at this point was a handful of staff officers and a single field piece. That one gun barked its defiance, and Gregg hesitated. His hesitation gave Stuart the time he needed to reorient his forces to deal with this new threat.

With the battle now fully joined, the conflict dissolved into a confusing melee of attacks and counterattacks. Units became intermingled and dust and smoke filled the battlefield. For the only time in the war, a large scale cavalry action imitated the depictions of it so popular in Harper's Weekly and other illustrated periodicals—sabers rose and fell, and horses wheeled, as men fought hand to hand. The fight lasted all morning and into the afternoon. By the narrowest of margins, Stuart managed to retain possession of Fleetwood Hill, and with Confederate infantry approaching, Pleasanton decided to call off the attack. The Federals withdrew in good order.

Both sides claimed victory. Pleasanton's claim was based on the fact that for the first time in the war Federal cavalry had fought rebel cavalry to a standstill. For his part, Stuart noted that the Confederates had driven off the enemy and that they held the field afterward. But there was no disguising the fact that he had been caught by surprise. The memory of that embarrassment would affect his actions in important ways during the subsequent campaign.

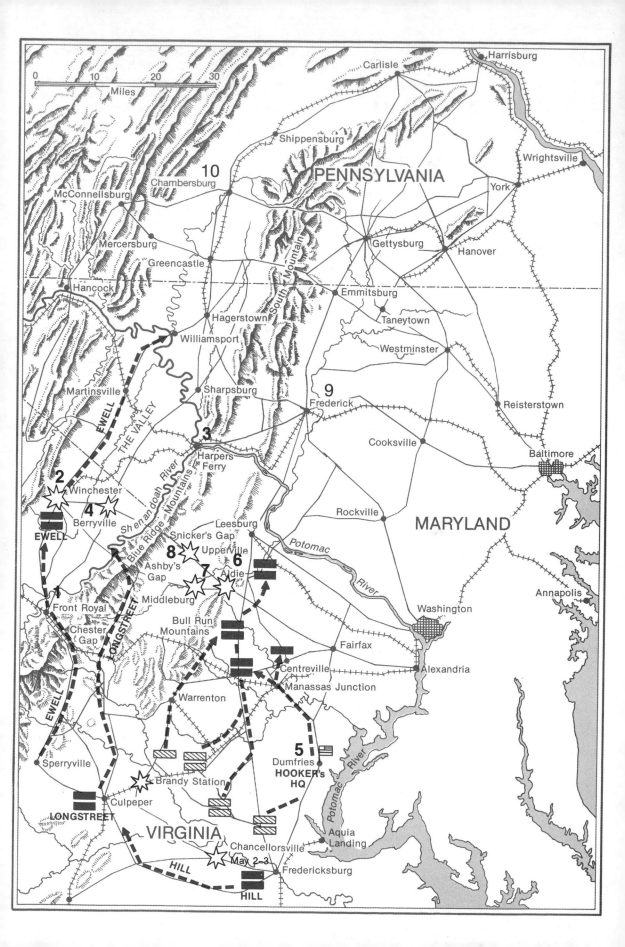

MAP 3

The Valley

June 10–June 28

The Shenandoah Valley is a picturesque swale of rolling farmland nestled between the Blue Ridge and the Shenandoah Mountains. From Front Royal (1), where the North and South forks of the Shenandoah River come together, for forty miles northward to Harpers Ferry, the Valley seemed made to accomodate an invading army from Virginia. Not only were the roads flat and straight, but the Blue Ridge Mountains to the east constituted a natural fence to screen military movements from the prying eyes of Federal cavalry. On the day after the fight at Brandy Station, the men of Ewell's Second Corps marched out of Culpeper and tramped westward through Sperryville and Chester Gap into the Shenandoah Valley near Front Royal. There they turned north and by June 13, they were on the outskirts of Winchester (2).

The Federal officer charged with the defense of the Shenandoah Valley was Major General Robert C. Schenck, who held that post largely because of his staunch support of Lincoln in the 1860 election. Schenck had positioned Major General Robert H. Milroy's 9,000-man division at Winchester as an outpost for the defense of Harpers Ferry (3). Halleck and Hooker—and even Lincoln—had warned Schenck that Milroy was too exposed at Winchester, but Schenck had ignored these warnings. On June 14, Ewell deployed his corps to surround Winchester and pluck Milroy's force like a ripe plum. Recognizing his danger too late, Milroy tried to fight his way out, but Ewell attacked him at Stephenson's Depot north of Winchester, taking some 4,000 prisoners and half a dozen field pieces. The rest of Milroy's command broke apart; one element fled all the way into Pennsylvania before halting. The next day at Berryville (4), Ewell's men took more prisoners and a cache of valuable supplies.

These events did little to improve Hooker's state of mind. Since Lincoln had rejected his proposal to cross the Rappahannock and attack Hill, Hooker believed his only remaining option was to shift his position back from the Rappahannock to stay between Lee's army and Washington. He withdrew four corps from the upper Rappahannock to Manassas Junction on June 13 (as Ewell was closing in on Winchester), and established his new headquarters at Dumfries (5). Hooker's nerves, perhaps still frayed by his experience at Chancellorsville, were tested further by his lack of precise intelligence about where the various elements of Lee's infantry were, and where they were going. On June 17, he ordered Pleasanton to send three brigades of cavalry toward the gaps in the Blue Ridge to find out what he could about enemy movements. "It is better that we should lose men," he wrote, "than to be without knowledge of the enemy."

The result was a series of cavalry skirmishes at Aldie (6) and nearby Middleburg (7). Four days later, Pleasanton struck again at Upperville (8), driving Stuart's men from the town and back toward Ashby's Gap. But although the Federal cavalrymen once again proved their mettle, they were unable to penetrate Stuart's cavalry screen to learn anything definitive about the Confederate infantry.

What Hooker *did* know was that at least part of Lee's army was at Winchester while another part of it was still at Culpeper. Lincoln suggested that since the rebel army was apparently strung out over at least 100 miles, "the animal must be very slim somewhere. Could you not break him?" But Hooker was not thinking of offensive action. Instead, he continued his complaints to Washington. He exaggerated the size of Lee's army, and seemed unwilling to accept the burden of command responsibility. For a week (June 17 to June 24), while Lee's infantry marched northward, Hooker kept the Army of the Potomac in the vicinity of the Bull Run Mountains. Finally on June 24, he issued orders for the army to move north to Frederick, Maryland (9). That same day, the lead elements of Lee's army reached Chambersburg, Pennsylvania (10).

Throughout this period, Hooker complained that the administration did not support him. As if determined to pick a quarrel, he wired Halleck that because he was outnumbered, he needed every available man in the field. He urged that Harpers Ferry be abandoned so that its garrison could be added to his field force. On June 27, Hooker visited Harpers Ferry to look over the situation for himself, and while he was there he received Halleck's reply that Harpers Ferry should not be abandoned unless it was absolutely necessary. Unreasonably irritated by this reply, Hooker sent in his resignation, no doubt expecting Halleck to back down. Instead it was accepted. The next day a courier arrived in the Federal camp with orders for George Gordon Meade to assume command of the army. For better or for worse, the Army of the Potomac would go north under yet another new commander.

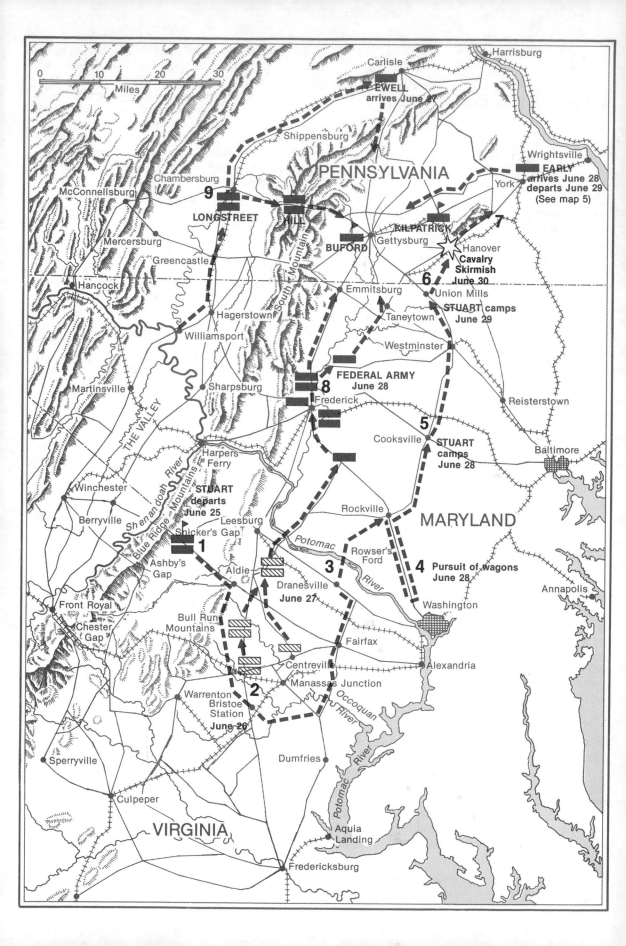

MAP 4

Stuart's Raid

June 25–June 30

Having successfully defended the passes through the Blue Ridge, Stuart was now free to contemplate his next move. As early as June 22 he wrote to Lee to ask guidance for the next phase of the campaign. He received Lee's answer the following day. Since so much subsequent debate centered on this dispatch, it is worth quoting the crucial passage:

> If you find that he [the enemy] is moving northward, and that two brigades can guard the Blue Ridge & take care of your rear, you can move with the other three into Maryland & take position on General Ewell's right, place yourself in communication with him, guard his flank, keep him informed of the enemy's movements & collect all the supplies you can for use of the army.

Stuart's overall task remained the same: to screen the infantry and provide Ewell with intelligence of enemy movements. But Lee had said nothing about the route that Stuart should take; it was characteristic of Lee to provide his commanders with general guidance rather than explicit instructions. Almost certainly, Lee expected that Stuart would fall back westward through Snicker's Gap (1) and ride past Longstreet's infantry through the Shenandoah Valley into Maryland. Alternatively, he might parallel the infantry's movement while staying on the eastern side of the ridge. But Stuart had another idea. Twice before Stuart had gained fame and glory by conducting dramatic cavalry raids completely around the Federal army, and he decided to do it again. It is at least possible that the disappointments of Brandy Station and Upperville made him eager for an opportunity to reassert the superiority of the Confederate cavalry and restore his own reputation. Then, too, Longstreet's endorsement to Lee's orders had implied that Stuart should at least consider such a raid.

Stuart therefore detailed the brigades of Beverly Robertson and ''Grumble'' Jones to guard the passes through the Blue Ridge, and ordered the other three, those of Wade Hampton, Fitz Lee, and John R. Chambliss, to prepare to ride eastward. His raid would have to be swift, for his assignment to guard Ewell's flank meant that he could not be out of contact from the infantry for very long.

Stuart left with his three brigades on June 25 and straight away he ran into trouble. His vedettes reported that a corps of Federal infantry was occupying the road from Aldie to Fairfax that Stuart had designated for the first leg of the raid. Stuart therefore chose another, more southerly route to avoid contact. The long line of gray-clad troopers turned southeast toward Bristoe Station (2), then swung east to cross the Occoquan River, before bending northward to Fairfax Court House. They crossed the Potomac at Rowser's Ford (3) early on the morning of June 28.

Across the river at Rockville, the rebel raiders chanced upon an irresistible prize: a train of 150 Federal wagons, fully loaded. The Federal wagon masters tried to escape by whipping their teams into a gallop, dashing down the Rockville Pike toward Washington, but Stuart's men came whooping after them and easily captured 125 of the wagons (4). By the time Stuart had his men re-formed, with the captured wagons in tow, much of the day was spent. They camped that night near Cooksville (5) in central Maryland. That same night, Ewell's infantry corps, the flank of which Stuart was supposed to guard, was more than a hundred miles to the north divided between Carlisle and York (see MAP #5).

Knowing that he was dangerously behind schedule, and encumbered now by his 125 captured wagons, Stuart started north the next day (June 29) to look for Ewell. His troopers covered thirty miles that day camping at Union Mills (6), but the next day they got only as far as Hanover, where they encountered a Federal cavalry division under Judson Kilpatrick (7). Both Yankees and Rebels were startled to see one another. Stuart was nearly taken prisoner, and had to escape by jumping his prize mare Virginia over a deep gully. With Kilpatrick occupying Hanover, the direct route to Gettysburg (only twelve miles away) was blocked, and Stuart decided to detour again, turning northeastward toward York.

Stuart's men had spent five days in the saddle, and during that time their commander had been unable to send any information about Federal movements to Lee. Even as Stuart led his three brigades toward York, the Confederate infantry was converging on Gettysburg unsure of the location or strength of the enemy. On July 1, the first day of the Battle of Gettysburg, Lee muttered to his staff, ''I cannot think what has become of Stuart; I ought to have heard from him long before now.''

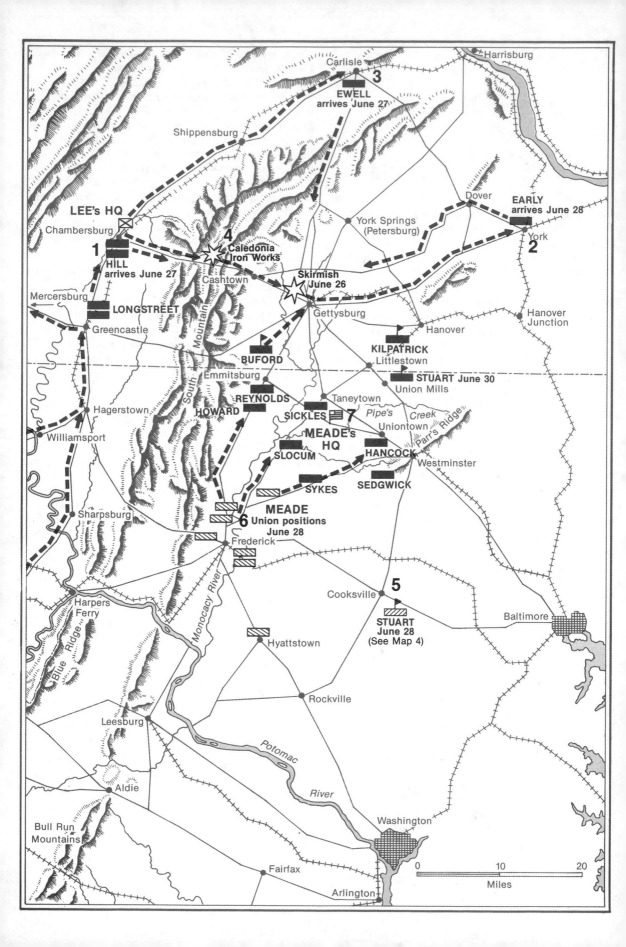

Harrisburg

Carlisle
3
EWELL
arrives June 27

Shippensburg

Dover

EARLY
arrives June 28

York Springs
(Petersburg)

York
2

LEE's HQ

Chambersburg

4
Caledonia
Iron Works

Hanover
Junction

1

HILL
arrives June 27

Cashtown

Skirmish
June 26

Mercersburg

LONGSTREET

Gettysburg

Hanover

Greencastle

KILPATRICK

Littlestown

STUART June 30

BUFORD

Emmitsburg

Union Mills

Hagerstown

REYNOLDS

Taneytown

HOWARD

Pipe's

Creek

Williamsport

SICKLES **7**

MEADE's
HQ

Uniontown

Parr's Ridge

Sharpsburg

SLOCUM

HANCOCK

Westminster

SYKES

SEDGWICK

6

MEADE
Union positions
June 28

Frederick

Monocacy River

Harpers
Ferry

5
Cooksville

Baltimore

Hyattstown

STUART
June 28
(See Map 4)

Blue Ridge

Rockville

Leesburg

Potomac

Aldie

River

Bull Run
Mountains

Washington

0   10   20

Miles

Fairfax

Arlington

MAP 5

The Invasion of Pennsylvania

June 24–28

While Stuart embarked on his cavalry raid, and Hooker complained dispiritedly to Washington, the gray-clad veterans of Ewell's corps crossed the Potomac at Williamsport and Shepherdstown, and strode northward along parallel roads to the vicinity of Chambersburg (1). En route, Ewell divided his forces, sending small units off to Mercersburg and McConnellsburg to the west, and dispatching Early's entire division with orders to march eastward through Gettysburg to York (2). Early's assignment was to cut the rail and telegraph lines between Baltimore and Harrisburg, and to burn the bridge over the Susquehanna at Wrightsville. Afterward, he was to rejoin Ewell at Carlisle (3).

En route to York, Early could not resist destroying the Caledonia Iron Works (4), which belonged to Pennsylvania Radical Congressman Thaddeus Stevens, even though this was a violation of Lee's orders to respect private property and to pay for any supplies gathered along the way. Outside Gettysburg on June 26, Early brushed aside a newly-formed regiment of Pennsylvania militia, and two days later (June 28), his infantry occupied York.

While Early marched west, the rest of Ewell's corps headed northwest through Shippensburg to Carlisle (3) where it arrived on June 27. At the same time, the lead elements of A.P. Hill's corps entered Chambersburg with Longstreet's men not far behind. That day too, Lee crossed the Mason Dixon line into Pennsylvania and set up his headquarters in Chambersburg. From there he issued General Order No. 73 congratulating the troops on their conduct and urging them to avoid "the barbarous outrages . . . and wanton destruction of private property that have marked the course of the enemy in our country." Many Pennsylvanians had feared that the rebels would plunder their farms and set fire to whatever they could not carry away. Rape and murder did not seem unlikely from these soldiers of the slavocracy. When it became apparent that this was not to be, the locals were so relieved, they barely complained when Lee's purchasing agents demanded that the towns produce a speci-

fied list of supplies and then "bought" those supplies with worthless Confederate money.

By June 28, the Confederate army was disposed in a sixty mile arc from Chambersburg through Carlisle, to York. Stuart, however, was still in central Maryland at Cooksville (5), and Lee had not heard from him for more than a week. That night, however, a paid spy named James Harrison, hired previously by Longstreet, brought Lee the intelligence that the Federal army was north of the Potomac and concentrated in the vicinity of Frederick (6). This should not have been a surprise to Lee; after all, his whole campaign was based on the assumption that the Federal army would have to follow him into Pennsylvania. But because he had not heard from Stuart, Lee assumed that the Federals must still be south of the Potomac. Now that he knew otherwise, he could no longer allow his army to remain spread out over sixty miles of Pennsylvania countryside. He immediately issued orders for the army to concentrate near Cashtown, five miles west of Gettysburg.

That same morning, thirty-five miles to the south, George Gordon Meade was awakened at three a.m. by a courier from Washington who handed him an order placing him in command of the Army of the Potomac. Meade was not altogether happy with his orders, but he accepted the assignment as a duty. With little time to adjust to his new responsibilities, he determined to head north and east to seek a confrontation with the enemy. He got the army off to an early start on June 29, but the soldiers were already tired from three days of hard marching, and there was much complaining and some straggling. At least the weather cooperated: it was drizzly much of the day, and the gentle rain cut the heat without ruining the roads. By nightfall, the army had moved twenty miles northward to the vicinity of Middleburg in northern Maryland (7). The lead infantry unit was Reynolds' First Corps which reached Emmitsburg that night, as did Howard's unlucky Eleventh Corps. On their right flank, half way to Westminster where Stuart's cavalry was resting, was Hancock's Second Corps.

That same day, Pleasanton sent cavalry probes out in advance of the infantry to discover what they could about the location of the rebel army. He sent two brigades under David McM. Gregg off to the right, toward Westminster, Maryland; he dispatched the division of Judson Kilpatrick toward Littlestown and his accidental encounter with Stuart at Hanover (see MAP #4); and he ordered John Buford to take two brigades from Fairfield toward Gettysburg. Buford's troopers cantered into Gettysburg just before noon on June 30.

the Death of Reynolds
at Gettysburg

THE FIRST DAY

July 1, 1863

It was the converging network of roads that made Gettysburg the destination of so many thousands of marching feet in the last few days of June, 1863. Like spokes to the hub of a wheel, no fewer than ten roads converged on Gettysburg: from Mummasburg, Carlisle, and Heidlersburg to the north; from York and Hanover to the east; from Baltimore, Taneytown, and Emmitsburg to the south; and from Hagerstown and Chambersburg to the west. The seat of Adams County with a population of about 2,400, Gettysburg had no industries or other strategic targets—the Confederates who passed through town four days before and had found nothing more useful than horseshoes and nails. Neither was it a center of commerce, boasting only the dead end of a minor railroad spur from Hanover, though the spade work for the continuation of that railroad to Chambersburg cut an ugly scar alongside the Chambersburg Pike west of town. Nevertheless, when Lee issued orders to bring his scattered units together, the road network compelled him to select Gettysburg. For Meade, too,

John F. Reynolds hurried his corps forward to Gettysburg in time to meet the attack of Heth's division on McPherson's Ridge on July 1. He did not live to see the outcome of the fight, however, as he fell victim to a Confederate minie ball. This sketch of the moment of his death is by Alfred Waud and is based on an eyewitness report. (Library of Congress)

moving cautiously northward, the roads led, perhaps inevitably, to Gettysburg.

The conflict at Gettysburg, which filled three days with some of the bloodiest fighting of a very bloody war, began innocuously enough with a hunt for shoes. On the morning of June 30, a Confederate infantry brigade commanded by John J. Pettigrew, moving eastward in advance of A. P. Hill's corps on the pike from Chambersburg, approached Gettysburg in a search for supplies. Rumor had led them to believe that shoes might be found there, and to the foot-weary rebel infantryman, shoes were as valuable as food or drink. Pettigrew halted his advance on the heights of Seminary Ridge at a little after 10:00 and examined the town through his field glasses. Off to his right he made out a long line of blue-coated cavalry riding into town from the south. Since he had come to forage and not to fight, he ordered his troops back onto the Pike and headed back the way he had come.

What Pettigrew had seen was the Union cavalry division of John Buford, veterans of Brandy Station, who cantered into Gettysburg from the south at about 11:00. Buford found the town in "a terrible state of excitement." Pointing westward up the Chambersburg Pike, the townspeople hurried to tell him that the rebels had just left. Not only that, other rebels had passed through town heading east four days earlier. Buford's troopers were tired and saddle sore—"fagged out" in Buford's own

George Gordon Meade inherited command of the Army of the Potomac only days before the Battle of Gettysburg. Though criticized by some as too willing to rely on the advise of his corps commanders, his bold decision to move the army northward and contest the crossroads at Gettysburg brought on the fight. (National Archives)

phrase—so he ordered them to dismount and rest while he sent scouting parties to the north and west. Late that night the scouting parties returned to report that there were indeed Confederates on the Chambersburg Pike: A. P. Hill's entire Confederate infantry corps was less than a day's march to the west at Cashtown, only nine miles away. Worse, rumor had it that another rebel corps, Ewell's, was on its way south from Carlisle, though his scouts could not confirm that. Buford's 3,000 tired troopers were apparently at the center of a closing vice with perhaps 50,000 men converging on them. Buford immediately sent reports of his discovery to Meade's headquarters, and also to Major General John F. Reynolds, commander of the First Corps, the clos-

est Union infantry unit, eleven miles to the south at Emmitsburg.

Reynolds got the news first. A twenty year veteran of the regular army, Reynolds had been Commandant of Cadets when the war broke out, and more than a few of those who now served under him remembered him as the exalted "Comm" of West Point. Meade had picked Reynolds to command not only the First Corps, but also to direct the movements of Sickles' Third Corps and Howard's Eleventh Corps. In effect, Reynolds commanded a third of the Union army. With Buford's report in his hands, Reynolds concluded that Lee was concentrating his army at Gettysburg, from which place he was likely to launch an attack southward. Reynolds therefore placed his own forces in a defensive posture facing north and suggested to Meade that the army make a stand at Emmitsburg.

Meade, who was another dozen miles to the south at Middleburg, soon had both Buford's report and Reynolds' recommendation. The burden of responsibility was his, and it weighed heavily on him. He wrote his wife that night that he was "much oppressed with a sense of responsibility and the magnitude of the great interests entrusted [to] me." There were three possible options: to advance quickly to Gettysburg and contest the cross-roads with Lee's converging columns; to take up a defensive position at Emmitsburg and challenge Lee to attack him; or to fall back to an even better position, a piece of high ground known as Parr Ridge behind Pipe's Creek (see MAP #5). All night he wrestled with the issue;

he could not decide. His staff prepared two sets of orders: one to advance, one to fall back to Pipe's Creek. Sometime before dawn, Meade reached his decision and issued orders for the army to advance to Gettysburg. The First and Eleventh Corps would march directly up the Emmitsburg Road; four other corps were to move within supporting distance. Rather than accept the defensive, Meade would advance to seize the crossroads.

Twenty miles to the north, Confederate commanders were making a similar decision. Pettigrew's men returned from their expedition to report to Harry Heth, the division commander, that they had seen Union cavalry in Gettysburg. Not home guard units, either, they insisted, but Army of the Potomac veterans.

Harry Heth graduated from West Point at the bottom of his class in 1847, and served 14 years at various frontier posts before the outbreak of the Civil War elevated him to command responsibility. His actions on July 1 suggest that he took the presence of Federal troops in Gettysburg altogether too lightly. (Library of Congress)

The bodies of Union soldiers from the Iron Brigade blanket the slope of McPherson's Ridge. These were members of the 24th Michigan regiment which lost more than 80% of its complement in the day's fight. McPherson's Woods are visible in the background. (Library of Congress)

Heth reported the information to A. P. Hill, who was skeptical. Just the day before, Lee had told him that the latest information showed that Meade was still at Middleburg. If there were Yankee regulars in Gettysburg, Hill suggested that it was probably a detached "squadron of observation." That being the case, Heth replied, would the general have any objections to his marching back to Gettysburg the next day? "None in the world," Hill replied.

When the first streaks of dawn struck the brick buildings and white spire of the Lutheran Seminary on July 1 (a Wednesday), the residents of Gettysburg could hardly have guessed that more than 140,000 armed men were converging on them from five directions. After the fact, at least one witness recalled that it was "a blood red sunrise," but perhaps this was poetic license exercised in consideration of the events of the day.

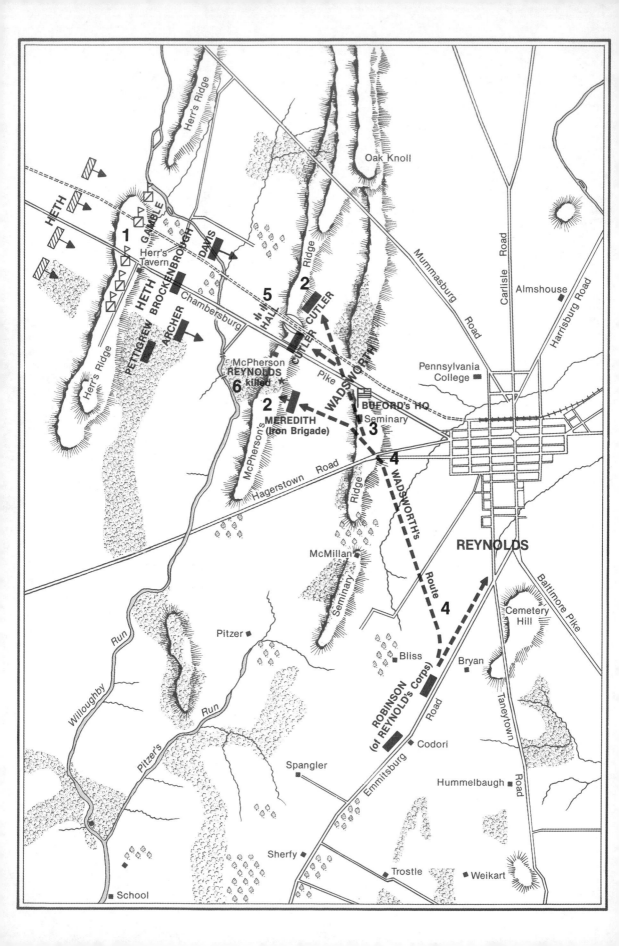

MAP 6

McPherson's Ridge

5:00 a.m. - 10:15 a.m.

Pettigrew's men were up before dawn on July 1 and by five a.m. they were on the road back to Gettysburg. This time they were accompanied by three more brigades—those of James J. Archer, J. M. Brockenbrough, and Joseph R. Davis—Heth's entire division of some 7,500 men. Only a few miles out of Cashtown, they encountered the vedettes Buford had posted there to keep him informed of enemy movements. The blue-coated riders took a long look at the marching column, wheeled, and spurred off down the road to carry the news to Buford.

Heth was not concerned. He did not believe there was any force in front of him more threatening than a scouting party. His disdain was partly justified. Waiting west of Gettysburg was a single brigade of cavalry—the 1,200 men of Brigadier General William Gamble's brigade (1). The rest of Buford's division was north and east of town on the look out for Ewell's men. But Gamble's troopers were well equipped and well placed. They carried the breech-loading Sharps rifle, faster and easier to load than the muzzle loaders carried by all infantry. Moreover, they occupied a good position, holding the crest of Herr's Ridge, a modest rise about two miles west of town. Even so, a brigade of cavalry could not expect to hold any position very long against a determined attack by a division of infantry.

At eight o'clock, Heth ordered his men to deploy; they drove in the Federal skirmishers and advanced. The Federals fought well, putting out an impressive volume of fire from their breech-loading weapons, but they were heavily outnumbered, and they soon fell back to McPherson's Ridge (2), another rise of open ground a mile closer to town. There, they stiffened and held. For nearly two hours, the Union cavalrymen held off an infantry force more than double their number. But they could not do so indefinately.

A little before ten o'clock, as the situation was becomming truly desperate, Buford saw General Reynolds and his staff gallop up to his headquarters at the Lutheran Seminary on Seminary Ridge (3).

Reynolds had received Meade's order to advance toward Gettysburg at four o'clock that morning, an hour before Heth started his division toward the town. But Meade had not suggested a particular need for urgency, and Reynolds' men did not start out on the road north until eight, about the time that Heth was beginning his attack. The lead unit in Reynolds' column was Major General James Wadsworth's First Division which included the "Iron Brigade," commanded by Solomon Meredith and composed of Midwesterners who celebrated their distinctiveness by wearing broad-brimmed black hats in place of the regulation kepi.

Riding at the head of the column, Reynolds was only two miles south of Gettysburg when a messenger from Buford brought word that the enemy was advancing in force. Soon afterward the unmistakeable low rumbling sound of artillery reached his ears. Now the need for haste was evident. Sending word to Wadsworth to close up and quicken the pace, Reynolds spurred his horse into a gallop and rode ahead with his staff toward the sound of the firing. He reined up at Buford's headquarters at the Lutheran Seminary just before ten. "What's the matter, John," he called informally. Buford replied in the same spirit: "The devil's to pay!" Reynolds asked Buford if he could hold his position until the infantry came up. "I reckon I can," Buford told him, and Reynolds raced back to hurry his troops along. En route he ordered his staff to tear down the fences between the Emmitsburg Road and McPherson's Ridge (4); the men would abandon the road and march cross country to save precious minutes.

Marching at the quick step, Wadsworth's men passed over Seminary Ridge and then across fields of ripening corn to McPherson's Ridge. They arrived just at the crisis moment. The hard-pressed cavalrymen were giving way, and to halt the Confederate momentum, Reynolds ordered the six gun battery of Captain Daniel Hall into action 100 yards in front of the ridge alongside the Pike (5). Well-placed rounds of packed cannister at close range compelled the rebels to slow their advance. Then the Federal infantry deployed into line. Reynolds waved the Iron Brigade into battle shouting "Forward men, forward for God's sake. . . ." They charged past him into McPherson's Woods (6). Only moments later, at about 10:15, Reynolds was struck by a minie ball and thrown from his saddle. His orderly jumped to the ground to assist him, but Reynolds was dead, killed instantly by a bullet to the head. He had arrived in time, but the battle would go on without him.

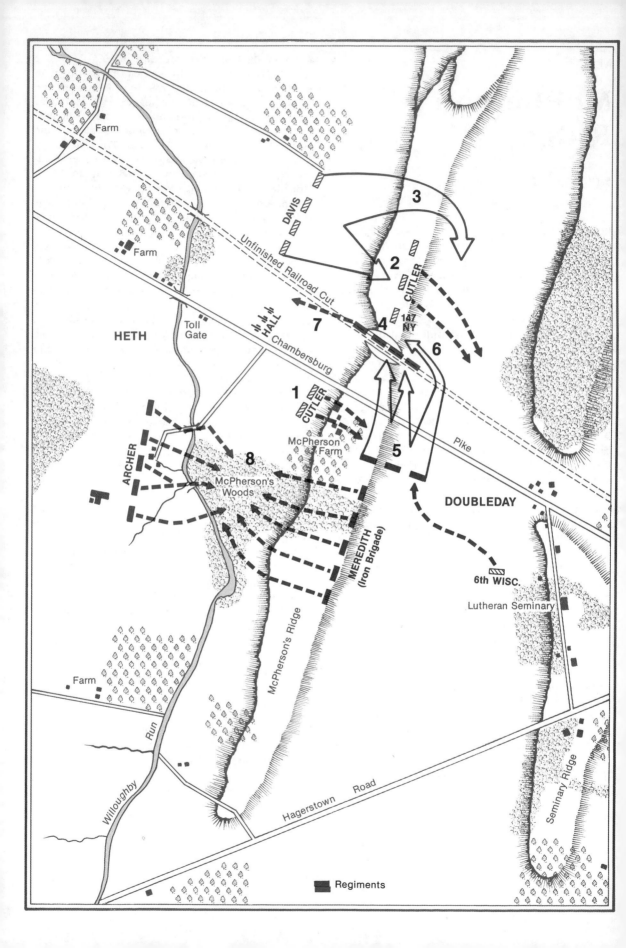

MAP 7

The Railroad Cut & McPherson's Woods

10:15 - 11:00 a.m.

With /Reynolds' death, command of the Union forces on McPherson's Ridge devolved upon Abner Doubleday. For the moment, however, there was little for him to do. Before he died, Reynolds had ordered the lead brigade of Wadsworth's Division, that of Lysander Cutler, to deploy his five regiments astride the Chambersburg Pike, and his last act in life had been to send the Iron Brigade under Meredith to drive the Confederates out of McPherson's Woods.

In obediance to these orders, two of Cutler's five regiments went into action south of the Pike (1) in support of Hall's Maine battery which was still banging away at the Confederates. Three more went into action north of the Pike (2) where they ran headlong into a brigade of three regiments under the command of Joseph R Davis, nephew of the Confederate president. Casualties were horrific on both sides in this stand up fight atop the ridge; the 76th New York regiment suffered 63 percent killed and wounded in a half hour. Though neither side could break the other frontally, the somewhat longer line of the Confederates enabled the 55th North Carolina regiment to swing around Cutler's flank (3).

Watching from Seminary Ridge, Wadsworth decided that the whole Union position north of the Chambersburg Pike was not tenable, and he ordered Cutler to fall back. Unfortunately, only two of the regiments north of the Pike received these orders, and the 147th New York fought on alone. That unit, and Hall's Maine battery, now came under very heavy pressure, and before long they too had to withdraw lest they be surrounded. Davis' brigade followed in pursuit.

Only a few dozen yards north of the Chambersburg Pike, and running parallel to it, the grading for the unfinished railroad from Gettysburg to Cashtown made a deep cut through McPherson's Ridge. Davis's victorious Mississippians saw this cut as a ready- made trench from which to fend off any Yan-

kee counterattack. They therefore dashed forward and took possession of the cut facing southward (4).

Doubleday assigned the 6th Wisconsin, heretofore held in reserve, to join Cutler's remaining regiments, and together they charged northward, across the Chambersburg Pike, against the rebels in the cut (5). Confederate volleys cut holes in their ranks as they advanced, but the momentum of their attack forced the Mississippi troops back into the deepest part of the cut. The 6th Wisconsin charged across the cut at a low point east of the ridge and some of the attackers clambered up its northern rim (6) so that blue-coated soldiers looked down from two sides on hundreds of Confederates trapped inside. The 2nd Mississippi regiment surrendered almost intact, and the rest fled out of the western end of the cut (7).

As desperate as the fighting was north of the Pike, it was even more so to the south in McPherson's Woods. Just before he died, Reynolds had waved the Iron Brigade into the fight with orders to "drive those fellows out of those woods." The proud men of the Iron Brigade loaded their muskets and fixed bayonets as they ran. Only a stone's throw to the west, James J. Archer's brigade of Tennessee and Alabama troops was entering the woods from the west. These two crack units collided headlong (8). Though Archer's men got off the first volley, a terribly effective one which staggered the Union line and wounded Meredith, they suffered a shock of their own when they saw the black hats and recognized the Iron Brigade.

This time it was the Union line that overlapped the rebel flank. Near Willoughby Run two Union regiments swung around Archer's right and poured a volley into the Confederate flank. In vicious fighting Archer's brigade was driven back across the run. The Black Hats pursued them and took several hundred prisoners, including Archer himself who was taken to the rear under escort where he encountered Doubleday. Archer was an old friend of Doubleday's who greeted him warmly extending his hand. "Good morning, Archer!" he called cheerfully. "How are you? I am glad to see you." But Archer ignored the hand and muttered, "Well, I am not glad to see you, by a damn sight, Doubleday."

Despite the initial advantage of numbers and timing, the first Confederate assault along McPherson's Ridge had failed. Both north and south of the Chambersburg Pike, the Confederates had been forced to give way, and they had lost several hundred prisoners.

But fate was about to deal a new hand.

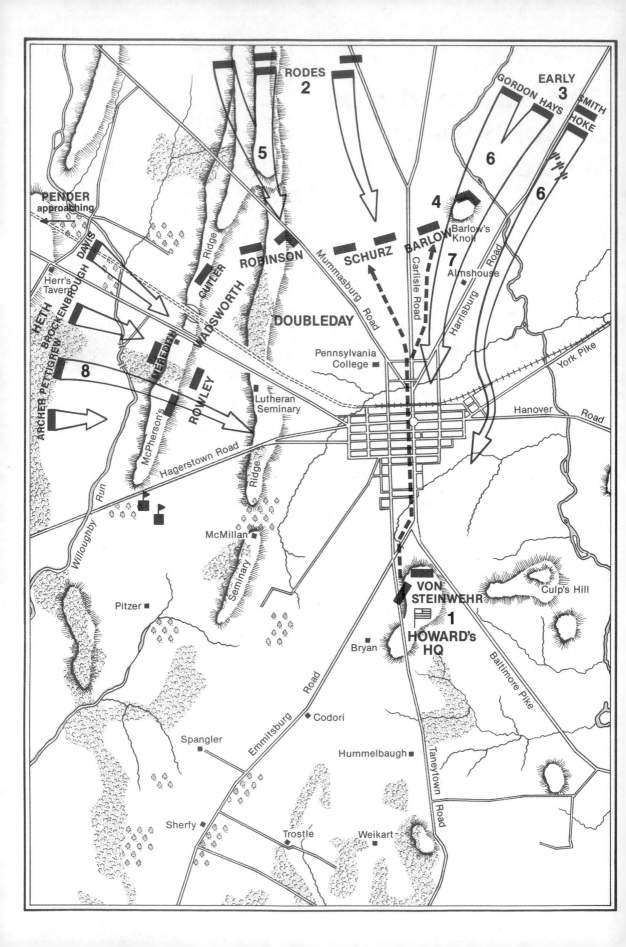

MAP 8

Ewell Breaks the Federal Line

12:00 noon - 3:30 p.m.

With Heth's repulse at about 11:00, the battlefield north and west of Gettysburg grew quiet. During the next few hours, while skirmishing continued along the banks of Willoughby Run, both sides brought up substantial reinforcements. Only two of Heth's four brigades had been heavily involved in the fight—Archer's and Davis'—and he now brought up the other two—those of Pettigrew and Brockenbrough. Moreover, Hill sent Dorsey Pender's division to his support giving the Confederates a total strength of nearly 15,000 men. For his part, Doubleday was happy to welcome the remaining two divisions of the Federal First Corps, those of John Robinson and Thomas Rowley, raising his strength to about 8,500, plus Buford's cavalry.

At the same time, Oliver O. Howard's Eleventh Corps (strength 9,500) was moving into Gettysburg from the south. Howard learned of Reynolds' death at about 11:30. Since Howard was the next senior corps commander, that put him, at least as he saw it, in command of the left wing of the army. He turned his own corps over to Carl Schurz, his senior division commander, and established his headquarters on Cemetery Hill south of town (1). He was still there at 12:30 when he received a message from Buford that new enemy forces were now gathering north of town on the right flank of Doubleday's position on McPherson's Ridge. These forces were the lead elements of Ewell's Corps: Robert Rodes' division marching south from Carlisle (2), and Jubal Early's division marching west from York (3), a total of another 15,000 men. Howard reacted to this news by sending two divisions of the Eleventh Corps, about 6,000 men, to form a line at right angles to Doubleday facing northward. Doubleday extended his right to the Mummasburg Road, placing Robinson's division there just south of the high ground known as Oak Ridge. The Federal defensive line formed a lazy L facing west and north. Howard kept one division, that of Adolph von Steinwehr, in reserve on Cemetery Hill.

The two Federal divisions which Howard placed north of Gettysburg occupied a very exposed position with few natural defensive barriers. Only a small knoll on the Federal right promised any defensive advantage, and to it Brigadier General Francis Barlow advanced two brigades (4). Though well placed for a defense against Rodes' division on Oak Ridge, this hill, still known as Barlow's Knoll, was vulnerable to a flank attack by Early's division arriving from the northeast.

At 2:30 the battlefield silence was broken when Rodes launched his 8,000-man division against Robinson's division of less than half that number (5). But the attack was not well coordinated, and despite their numerical advantage, the Confederates were thrown back. While Rodes rallied his men for another try at about 3:30, Early's division came into the fight on the Federal right (6) where John B. Gordon's Georgia brigade assailed Barlow's exposed flank at the knoll. Barlow himself fell wounded and was captured; his men stood their ground only briefly before fleeing the field, thus destroying the integrity of the Federal position. The remnants of Barlow's brigades attempted to rally at the Alms House on the Harrisburg Road (7), but they were broken again and fled southward. Now Rodes and the rest of Early's division advanced together, and the Federals north of town gave way in a rush, fleeing into the streets of Gettysburg—another humiliation for the Eleventh Corps.

On McPherson's Ridge, Doubleday's men continued to hold their position, but Schurz' retreat left Doubleday's right not only exposed, but in imminent danger of being enveloped. Seizing the opportunity, Heth launched a fresh attack led by Pettigrew's brigade (8). The Federals resisted fiercely, especially the Iron Brigade which did not want to quit McPherson's Woods, but gradually they were forced back to Seminary Ridge. There Pender's fresh troops passed through the ranks of Heth's exhausted soldiers to assail the Federals again. With no more than 2,500 men left of the 8,200 who had begun the fight, the First Corps continued its retreat through town, south to the heights of Cemetery Hill.

Confederate arms had won the field. It was not, however, strategic insight or tactical brilliance that had triumphed. The outnumbered and outgunned Union soldiers were broken by the timely arrival of Ewell's corps north of town on the Federal right flank at precisely the right time and place to overwhelm the Federal defensive line. Still, by fortune or by skill the rebels had clearly won the day and now it remained to be seen if they could harvest the fruits of victory.

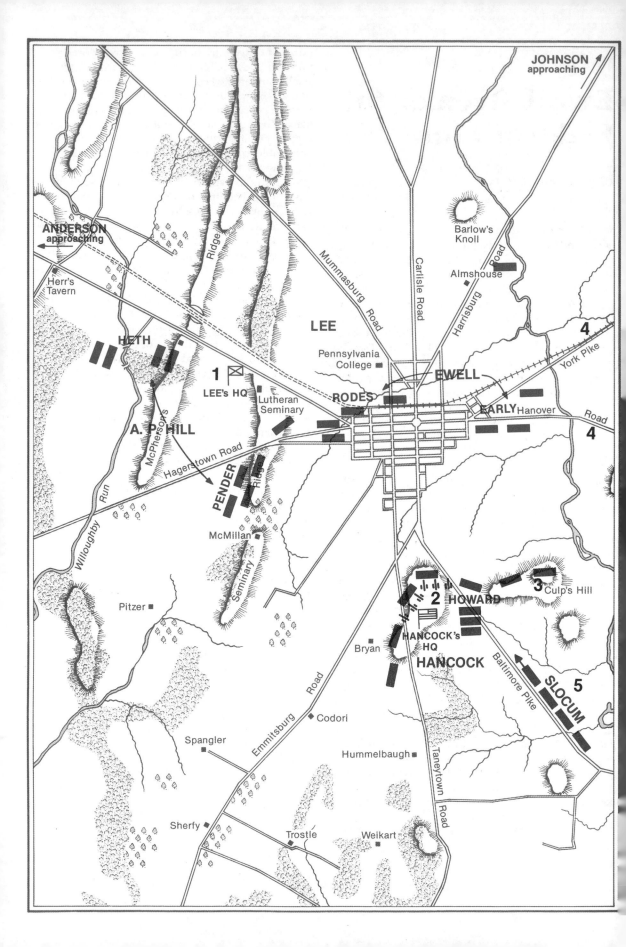

JOHNSON
approaching

ANDERSON
approaching

Herr's
Tavern

HETH

LEE

Pennsylvania
College

Barlow's
Knoll

Almshouse

4

EWELL

York Pike

RODES

EARLY Hanover Road

4

1

LEE's HQ

Lutheran
Seminary

A. P. HILL

McPherson's

Hagerstown Road

PENDER

Willoughby Run

McMillan

Seminary Ridge

Ridge

Pitzer

Culp's Hill

3

2 HOWARD

HANCOCK's
HQ

Bryan

HANCOCK

Baltimore Pike

SLOCUM

5

Emmitsburg Road

Codori

Spangler

Hummelbaugh

Taneytown Road

Sherfy

Trostle

Weikart

MAP 9

The Lost Opportunity

4:00 - 5:30 p.m.

The Confederate victory north and west of Gettysburg created both an opportunity and a dilemma for Robert E. Lee. He had entered Pennsylvania determined to avoid a general engagement until he could bring all three of his infantry corps together to deliver a knockout blow. He was not altogether pleased, therefore, when he arrived outside Gettysburg at 2:00 to find four of his nine divisions involved in a stand up fight with two Federal corps. When Heth rode up at 2:30 to ask permission to renew the action on McPherson's Ridge, Lee turned him down. "I am not prepared to bring on a general engagement today," he replied. "General Longstreet is not up." But despite his misgivings, he could see an opportunity when it was in front of him. At 4:30, from his new position on Seminary Ridge (1), Lee watched as Early and Rodes overwhelmed the Federals north of town, and he quickly ordered Heth to advance as well. At four o'clock it seemed that victory was within grasp.

At that moment, Federal Major General Winfield Scott Hancock was riding up to the top of Cemetery Hill (2). Hancock had been at Meade's headquarters at Middleburg when news arrived of Reynolds' death. Anxious to obtain a reliable assessment of the situation at Gettysburg, Meade sent Hancock to take command of the forces there and send him a report. Hancock arrived just as the survivors of the disaster north of town began to stream up onto the hill. Howard was disappointed to learn that he had been superseded, and reminded Hancock that he was, after all, senior in rank. In the end he accepted Hancock's authority and did his best to cooperate, though he protested to Meade in a private note that evening. Hancock and Howard set to work laying out defensive lines on Cemetery Hill, and later on Culp's Hill to the east (3). The Federals dug in, glancing anxiously northward from time to time to see if the Confederates were coming.

During this crucial hour from four to five, Lee considered the possibility that he could achieve something decisive after all. He asked A. P. Hill if his men were capable of one more push to carry them up and over Cemetery Hill, but Hill replied that the men of Heth's and Pender's divisions were exhausted and nearly out of ammunition; Anderson's division was too distant. Lee then sent his aide, Major Walter Taylor, to ask Ewell if he thought his divisions could storm the enemy position on Cemetery Hill. Lee did not order Ewell to do it; he left the final decision to his corps commander.

Ewell did not like the look of the Federal position, already crowned by Federal artillery, and because of the absence of Stuart's cavalry, he was unsure what other Federal forces might be on the York Pike or the Hanover Road in a position to threaten his left if he did attack (4). Besides, he did not anticipate the arrival of his own third division—that of Edward Johnson—until dark. In the end, he decided that an attack on Cemetery Hill was not practicable, and with his decision the first day's fight came to an end. Did Ewell miss an opportunity to finish off the Federal forces at Gettysburg before the rest of Meade's army arrived? In the years after the battle, his critics compiled a strong case. The Federal forces of the First and Eleventh Corps had been badly defeated—the First Corps suffered losses of nearly 70 percent in the day's fight. In addition, the Confederates retained a numerical advantage, a rare circumstance in the war. Finally, they had the sense of moral superiority which comes from seeing the backs of their enemy as the Federals fled through town.

Compelling as such arguments are, it is unlikely that an attack by Early's Division could have achieved the decisive results its advocates have suggested. First of all, the rebels had been on the offensive all day, and they had suffered too—at least 5,600 Confederate soldiers were killed or wounded that first day as compared to 5,400 Federals.* Second, as disorganized and demoralized as the Federals seemed at 4:00 when their defensive line collapsed, they were hardly a shattered force. Having gained the heights of Cemetery Hill where Hancock and Howard had stationed the Federal artillery, they recovered quickly and dug in. Hancock infused them with his own cheerful energy, and they were further cheered at 5:00 when the lead elements of Major General Henry W. Slocum's Twelfth Corps began to arrive (5). All this produced such a dramatic change that at 5:25 Hancock reported to Meade that his position "cannot well be taken."

Despite the tonic of victory, the Confederates were simply incapable of launching another attack in the gathering dusk. Instead, both armies went into bivouac knowing that the fight would be renewed the next day.

---

*See Appendix B.

THE SECOND DAY

July 2, 1863

For the exhausted troops who had survived the first day's fighting, the coming of night was a respite. The Federals who wearily climbed the gentle slope of Cemetery Hill to take refuge behind the Union guns had been beaten, but they had not been broken. Hancock's arrival and the promise of substantial reinforcements made them confident that they could turn the tables on their enemy the next day. The Confederates were equally tired, but having seen the backs of their enemy, they were bursting with confidence. The butternut-clad veterans who occupied the streets of Gettysburg at nightfall bragged openly to the townspeople that they would finish tomorrow what they had started that morning.

For the officers who bore the responsibility to plan the next day's fight there was no respite. Meade arrived on Cemetery Hill in the pre-dawn darkness of July 2 after a long ride from Taneytown. He dismounted at the gate to the Cemetery where three of his corps commanders met him. One volunteered his opinion that it was good ground for a fight. Meade tiredly replied, "It is just as well, for it is too late to leave." After further conversation with his officers, Meade remounted for a tour of the Federal position. At 2:00 a.m. he rode down the spine of Cemetery Ridge, past the huddled forms of sleeping soldiers, to the base of Little Round Top. Then he retraced his steps to Cemetery Hill and ascended Culp's Hill on the extreme right.

Meade was satisfied by what he saw on the Union left. Cemetery Ridge was hardly a dominating geographical feature—it was not even a ridge except by name, being only about a dozen feet higher than the ground in front of it, but from it the men of Hancock's recently-arrived Second Corps had a clear field of fire—some 12,400 of them occupied about a mile of front, a concentration of five men to the yard. Meade felt confident they could hold their position. The natural strength of Cemetery Hill manned by Howard's Eleventh Corps made the Federal center secure. Even if Howard's troops were not the best, they were likely to hold that strong point. Meade was most concerned about his right where Slocum's Twelfth Corps and the remnants of the First Corps guarded Culp's Hill. In his pre-dawn tour, he suggested to Slocum that there was a gap in the line at Rock Creek, and he ordered John Geary's division from Hancock's left near Little Round Top to fill it.

By now the sun was up—it rose at 4:15, a great orange ball in the eastern sky, promising another hot July day. By 7:00 the temperature was already 74 degrees and on its way into the nineties. Still, every minute that passed raised Meade's spirits, for his greatest fear was that

James Longstreet orders his division forward toward the Wheat Field and the Peach Orchard on the afternoon of July 2. Longstreet was reluctant to undertake the tactical offensive at Gettysburg, and his critics have charged him with deliberate foot-dragging. In this portrayal, however, he appears as Lee's "Old War Horse" gesturing toward the Round Tops in the background. (Library of Congress)

Daniel Sickles, commander of the Federal Third Corps, was a flamboyant personality. As a Congressman in 1859 he had shot his wife's lover to death in broad daylight in the nation's capital, only to be acquitted by pleading the "unwritten law." At Gettysburg, he decided that the slightly higher ground along the Emmitsburg Road was a better position than the one assigned him by Meade. Sickles lost a leg in the fight, which he had pickled and kept in a jar. (Library of Congress)

Lee would attack at dawn before the Federals were ready to receive him. Now that threat was past. By 8:00 Meade was positively cheerful, or at least as cheerful as he was capable of being. The longer Lee waited to attack, the better the Federal chances were.

Lee, too, had spent a busy and troubled night. He had arrived at Gettysburg on the afternoon of July 1 in time to witness the collapse of the Federal Eleventh Corps at 4:00 o'clock. An hour later while he watched the Federals digging in on Cemetery Hill, James Longstreet had ridden up to report. Lee was pleased to see him; with the arrival of Longstreet's Corps, the army would be united once again. Lee pointed out the Federal position on Cemetery Hill and encouraged Longstreet to look it over. In the gathering dusk, Longstreet examined it closely through his field glasses. According to Longstreet's postwar memoirs,

he then turned to Lee to exclaim: "All we have to do is throw our army around their left, and we shall interpose between the Federal army and Washington. . . . The Federals will be sure to attack us."

Longstreet and Lee had shared strategic views regularly on the long march up from Virginia, and from their conversations Longstreet was sure that Lee shared his own belief in the importance of fighting a defensive battle. Longstreet's experience at the Battle of Fredericksburg, where the Confederate army had waited behind a stone wall and slaughtered the Union troops as they charged, had helped settle his conviction that with the advent of the minie ball and its longer range, offensive tactics were no longer suitable except in rare circumstances. Now, to Longstreet's great dismay, Lee replied, "No. The enemy is there, and I am going to attack him

Gouverneur Warren looks over the battlefield from the crest of Little Round Top. Astonished to discover that only a small signal team occupied this crucial height, he directed two Federal brigades to occupy the high ground just in time to blunt Longstreet's attack. (National Archives)

there." Longstreet remonstrated, but Lee would not be moved. Quiet and unemotional, but also firm, he emphasized his determination to strike the enemy where he was.

After his conversation with Longstreet, Lee rode over to the left at about 8:00 p.m. to talk with Ewell and his division commanders. Could Ewell's men storm Cemetery Hill at daybreak? Lee asked. Whatever Ewell's answer might have been was overridden by Early's quick response that the ground around Cemetery Hill was too well suited to the defense to promise any decisive gains. Better, he suggested, to strike the enemy on the other flank, near the Round Tops. Ewell soberly confirmed his division commander's views.

Despite such tepid responses from Long-street and Ewell, by midnight Lee had formed a plan in his mind. He would attack, striking the Federal left flank near the Round Tops. Since Hill's Corps was worn out from the first day's fight, and Ewell's Corps was too far away on the Confederate left, Longstreet's fresh troops would spearhead the assault. Ewell would wait until he heard the sound of Longstreet's attack and then demonstrate against the Federal right. Meade's army might be caught in a classic pincer movement.

At 5:00 a.m. on July 2, less than an hour after sunrise, Lee and Longstreet were again side by side on Seminary Ridge studying the Federal lines. Lee outlined his plan and again Longstreet objected to undertaking an offensive, stating his case as forcefully as he could

[41]

Joshua Chamberlain commanded the 20th Maine regiment at Gettysburg. His cool leadership in the defense of Vincent's Spur won him the Congressional Medal of Honor. (National Archives)

No aspect of the Battle of Gettysburg has been more controversial than this disagreement between Lee and Longstreet. In the years since, each man has attracted his share of defenders. One interpretation is that Longstreet was so committed to the idea of a defensive fight that he deliberately dragged his feet when ordered to attack. According to this view, Longstreet was a reluctant warrior at Gettysburg whose reluctance upset the timetable of Lee's plans. After the war Longstreet openly criticized Lee's tactics at Gettysburg, suggesting in his memoirs that Lee was not fully in control of himself that day. Lee "was excited," Longstreet wrote, "and off his balance." He relented only when "enough blood was shed to appease him." Such words about

a man who was revered by the entire South and much of the North worked only to discredit the author.

But Longstreet has attracted his share of defenders as well. They suggest that Lee may very well have been "off his balance" that day, suffering not only from the understandable anxiety that would result from fighting a major battle deep in enemy territory without the comforting intelligence of Stuart's regular reports, but also from his intermittant heart problems. In his Pulitzer Prize winning novel *The Killer Angels,* Michael Shaara suggests that Lee was eager to bring things to a close quickly at Gettysburg because he feared that he could not carry the burden much longer. According to this interpretation, Lee seized on the chance offered at Gettysburg to win or lose it all on a single throw of the dice.

As in most such controversies, there is merit on both sides. But on the whole Lee was probably correct to seize the moment. Seldom in the war did the Army of Northern Virginia face such nearly equal odds. The conclusion of the most thoughtful student of the battle, Edwin Coddington, is that: "Never again would General Lee have as good an opportunity to defeat his old foe under conditions which might bring about the decisive military and political results he so eagerly sought."

As the sun rose to full height on July 2 and the temperature climbed, the armies of both sides poised themselves for a climactic confrontation.

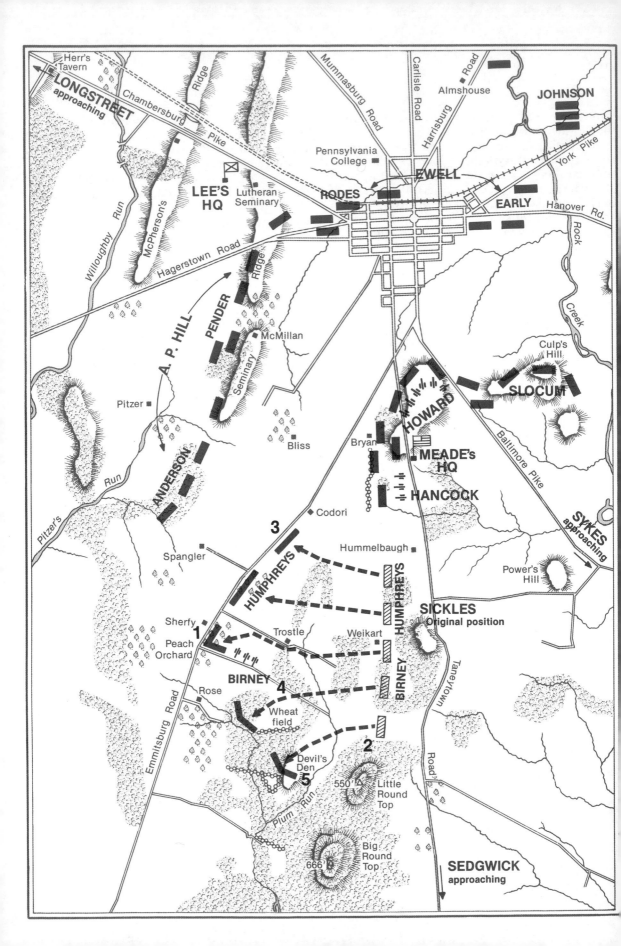

MAP 10

Sickles Moves Forward

9:00 a.m. - 3:00 p.m.

To Meade's great satisfaction, additional units of the Federal army continued to arrive at Gettysburg throughout the morning on July 2. The lead elements of Daniel Sickles' Third Corps marched up the Emmitsburg Road at around 9:00 o'clock, turning east toward Cemetery Ridge at the Peach Orchard (1). Though ordered to march to Gettysburg the night before, Sickles did not have his men on the road until 4:00 a.m. and they had covered only about nine miles in five hours. Still, here they were at last, and Meade directed Sickles to form his corps on Hancock's left extending the Union line to Little Round Top (2).

A New York Congressman before the war, Sickles owed his original appointment as brigadier general to the fact that he was a War Democrat with ties to Tammany Hall. Though he had performed well enough as a brigadier to gain promotion to major general, he was largely inexperienced as a corps commander. His lack of experience did not dampen his self-confidence, however. On the morning of July 2, as he looked around the position Meade had assigned him, he did not like the look of it. His left flank was completely unguarded—in the air as the saying went. Moreover, the ground to his front along the Emmitsburg Road was actually higher than his own. If the Confederates brought artillery to the high ground around the Peach Orchard, it could sweep his position. Though another officer might simply assume that Meade knew what he was doing, Sickles had more confidence in his own judgement than he did in Meade's.

At 10:00, therefore, Sickles rode to Meade's headquarters to argue that his corps should move forward to occupy the slightly higher ground to his front. He invited the commanding general to come view the position for himself. Meade declined; he had ridden over the ground eight hours before, and in any case he was busy. Sickles then asked if Meade would send a staff officer to look at the ground and Meade agreed to send Brigadier General Henry J.

Hunt. Back on Cemetery Ridge, Hunt agreed with Sickles that the ground along the Pike was slightly higher, especially near the Peach Orchard, but Hunt declined to authorize Sickles to change his position. After all, Sickles' was only one of seven Federal army corps, and the strength of his own position did not matter nearly as much as how it supported the overall Federal line.

Sickles was not satisfied. Soon after Hunt left him, he noted that Buford's cavalry, which had been guarding his front and flank, moved off to the rear in conformance with earlier orders. This made Sickles even more nervous for the security of his flank. He decided to send a company of sharpshooters forward to see what enemy forces, if any, were in the treeline along Seminary Ridge. The sharpshooters advanced at 1:00 and soon ran into a heavy concentration of rebels in the woods. As far as Sickles was concerned, that was decisive. At 2:00, he ordered David Birney's division to move forward to the high ground at the Peach Orchard, and an hour later he ordered A. A. Humphreys' division forward as well.

Sickles' new position jutted out from Cemetery Ridge at a thirty degree angle to run along the eastern edge of the Emmitsburg Road (3). At the high ground of the Peach Orchard, it turned ninety degrees to the left and ran along a farm road back toward a wheatfield (4). From there it followed a branch of Plum Run to a jumble of massive boulders that came to be known as the Devil's Den (5).

While Sickles was moving his divisions forward, the first elements of John Sedgwick's Sixth Corps began to arrive at Gettysburg after a hard march of some thirty four miles. Since the Sixth Corps was the largest in the army, Meade was especially pleased to see it. Feeling more secure than he had at any time since the night before, Meade finally rode south to inspect Sickles' position around 4:00 p.m. When he got there he was astonished to find that Sickles had thrust his corps forward to the Emmitsburg Road. Positively furious, Meade lost his famous temper. He turned and pointed back to Cemetery Ridge telling Sickles: That is where you should be! Sickles offered to move back at once, but Meade knew it was impossible. "I wish to God you could," he said, "but the enemy won't let you."

As if to underscore his words, a discharge of artillery not far off indicated that Lee was now, finally, beginning his attack, and his target was Sickles' exposed salient.

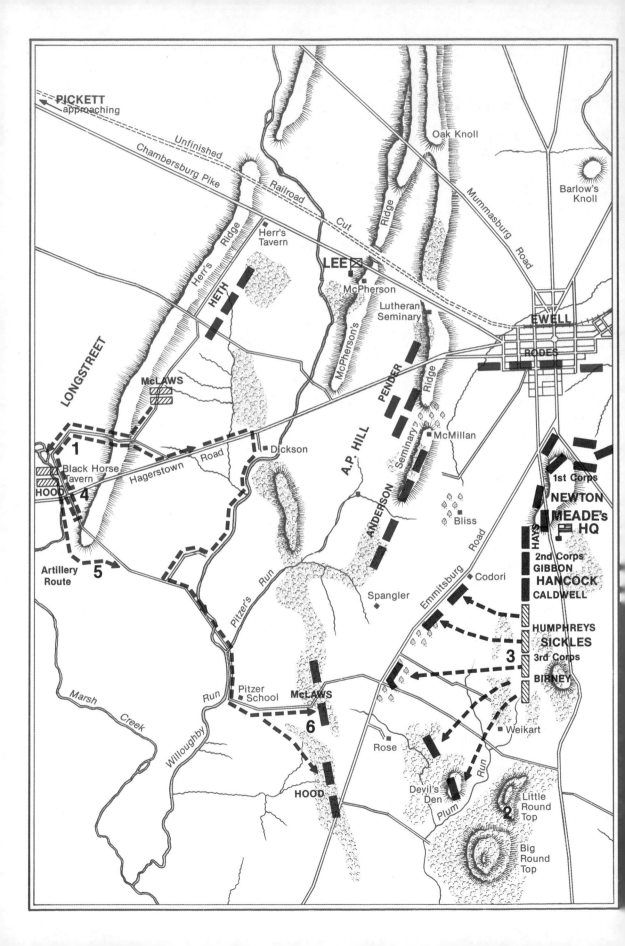

MAP 11

Longstreet's Approach

noon - 4:00 p.m.

James Longstreet was Lee's "Old War Horse." With Jackson's death, he had become Lee's most valued subordinate and his only experienced corps commander. Now it was Longstreet to whom Lee entrusted responsibility for the attack on the Federal left. Two of Longstreet's three divisions, those of John Bell Hood and Lafayette McLaws, had gone into bivouac along Marsh Creek the night before and were within easy marching distance (1). His third division—Pickett's—was still on the Chambersburg Pike and expected to arrive later that day.

Lee sent a scout from his own staff, Captain S. R. Johnston, to survey the ground and select a route for Longstreet's attack. Between 7:00 and 8:00 that morning, Johnston led a party of 200 men down Willoughby Run, across the Emmitsburg Road and up onto Little Round Top (2). Amazingly, he encountered not one enemy soldier. Johnston spurred his horse up to the crest of Little Round Top from which he could view nearly the entire Federal position away to the north. He returned to Confederate lines to report that the high ground was unoccupied. Only moments later, Sickles' men came marching up the Emmitsburg Road. The Confederates noted their arrival, but noted, too, that they went into position on Cemetery Ridge (3). The Federal left was still open to a flank attack.

Delighted with the news Johnston brought him, Lee turned to Longstreet and asked him to prepare the attack. Longstreet, however, was still unreconciled to an offensive, and he again raised several objections. Lee listened patiently, but he refused to modify his orders. Trusting in Longstreet's professionalism, Lee left him in charge of the arrangements while he rode off to Ewell's headquarters.

Lee returned two hours later at 11:00 and found all the soldiers still in their camps. Longstreet excused his lack of progress by explaining that he was waiting for the arrival of Pickett's Division. But it was already near noon, and Lee knew he could wait no longer. If Pickett was approaching, so too, were large numbers of Federal reinforcements. This time

Lee gave Longstreet his orders in no uncertain terms: His artillery was to occupy the high ground around the Peach Orchard, and under the cover of its fire, the infantry would attack up the Emmitsburg Road rolling up the Federal left as it advanced.

Longstreet's men finally began to move at noon, seven hours after Lee first ordered the attack. But even now there were unforeseen delays. McLaws' Division initially marched southward along the banks of Marsh Creek crossing the Fairfield Road near the Black Horse Tavern (4). But a few hundred yards beyond it, the farm road ascended a shoulder of Herr Ridge from which the column could be seen from Little Round Top where a Federal signal team was operating. Longstreet might have sent his troops around the shoulder of the ridge and kept them out of sight as E. P. Alexander's artillery did (5), but instead he chose to backtrack and take an alternate route. The troops countermarched, passed their own campsite, and headed north, crossing Herr Ridge behind the screen of the trees on Seminary Ridge. From there, the men followed Willoughby Run back to the original farm road. Instead of a half mile on a dirt road, they marched nearly four miles, much of it cross country.

While Longstreet's men followed this circuitous route, the men of Sickles' Corps were advancing to the Emmitsburg Road. Thus it was that when the men of McLaws' Division passed the Pitzer School and began to deploy just west of the Emmitsburg Road near the Peach Orchard (6), they found not an open flank, but a Federal corps arrayed in front of them. McLaws sent word back to Longstreet that a large body of Federal troops was in his front, but Longstreet dismissed the report, and told McLaws to go ahead with the attack. Hood, too, was disturbed by what he saw. In addition to substantial Federal forces, the terrain to his front was very rough— the huge boulders of Devil's Den and the rocky terrain around Plum Run were sure to impede his attack and aid the defenders. Moreover, Hood's scouts brought word that the Federal line did not extend beyond the Round Tops. Hood sent a message to Longstreet asking permission to swing around the end of the Federal line and attack the enemy in flank and rear. Longstreet would not hear of it. "General Lee's orders are to attack up the Emmitsburg Road." Hood was so disturbed by Longstreet's reply that he went in person to see him. Again Longstreet turned him down. "We must obey General Lee's orders," he said stubbornly. Resigned, Hood returned to his troops. At 4:00, McLaws' artillery opened fire, and the attack began.

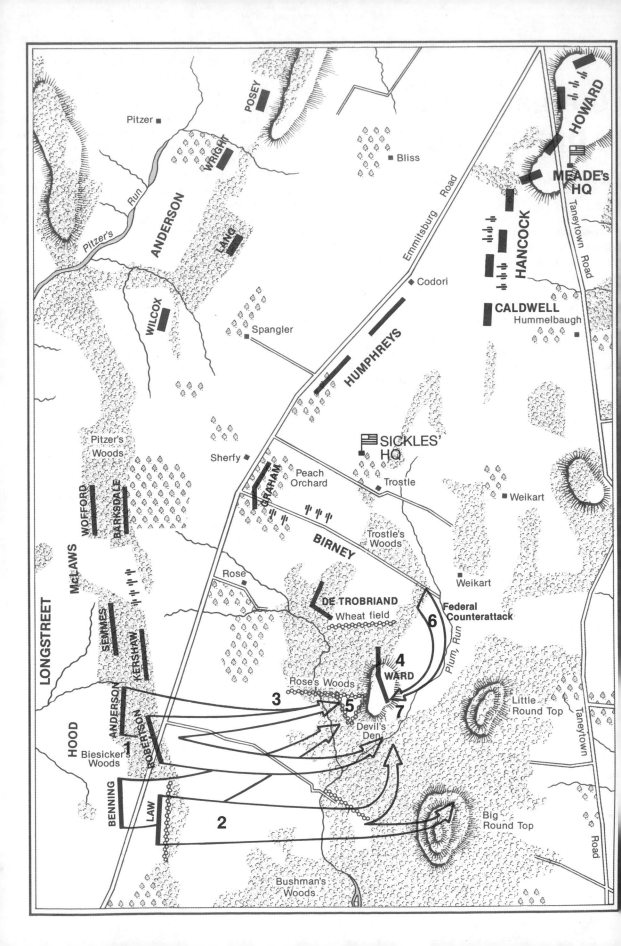

MAP 12

Devil's Den

4:00 - 5:00 p.m.

Lee's plan called for Longstreet's divisions to attack *en echelon,* that is, sequentially from right to left: Hood's division on the extreme right would attack first, followed by McLaws, and then by Anderson's division of A. P. Hill's corps. In this way, each division would screen the attack of the next, preventing the enemy from enfilading the attackers. Counting Anderson's Division, a total of some 21,000 Confederates would participate in the attack on the 8,000 men of Sickles' Corps.

After the roundabout march from Black Horse Tavern, Hood deployed his four brigades in Biesecker's Woods (1) with the two lead brigades straddling the Emmitsburg Road. The brigades of Evander Law (on the right) and John C. Robertson (on the left) occupied the front rank. Behind them Hood placed the brigades of Henry Benning and George Anderson. At four o'clock the Confederate artillery signalled the start of the attack. Hood rose in his stirrups and called for his men to fix bayonets, then he waved them forward with his drawn sword. His men answered with the rebel yell, and stepped out of the woods to the attack.

In Lee's conception, Hood's Division would advance on a line parallel to the Emmitsburg Road, but the attraction of the high ground of the Round Tops drew the attackers considerably to the right of this intended line of attack. Hood himself sent his troops off with the command to "take those heights" gesturing to Big Round Top a thousand yards away. As a result, Law's brigade attacked almost due east, perpendicular to the Emmitsburg Road (2). On Law's left, Robertson's Brigade was supposed to advance so that his left kept in contact with the road and his right with Law. But as Law pushed off further and further to the east, this became impossible. A wide gap appeared in the center of Robertson's attack formation as the two right hand regiments kept in contact with Law, and the two on the left marched northeasterly toward Rose's Woods and Devil's Den (3).

It was Hood's responsibility to coordinate the advance of the two brigades, but early in the attack a

Federal artillery shell burst near him, throwing him to the ground, and severely wounding him in his left arm. Losing blood rapidly, and probably in shock, he was helped to the rear and spent the rest of the afternoon in a hospital tent near the Pitzer School. Almost at once, therefore, responsibility for the conduct of the attack fell to the brigade and even regimental commanders.

The target of the Confederate onslaught was the Federal brigade of Brigadier General J. H. Hobart Ward (4), part of Birney's division of Sickles' Corps. Ward had five regiments on a line between the Devil's Den and a nearby wheatfield, plus eight companies of sharpshooters and a battery of four guns in Devil's Den itself. Watching the Confederate advance, Ward told his men to hold their fire until the enemy was within 200 yards. The Federals then fired a massed volley that staggered the attackers and forced them to take cover. The fight centered around a triangular piece of open rocky ground east of Devil's Den (5), a mountain meadow bounded by low rock walls and thick woods, which attackers and defenders alike used for cover. The Federals fought fiercely, surprising the Confederates with their determination. The 124th New York even counterattacked across the meadow, briefly driving the rebels into the woods before being themselves forced back. But the Federals were low on ammunition, and when Benning's Brigade joined Robertson's in the attack, the lone Union brigade was overwhelmed. The Confederates charged uphill into the Devil's Den capturing three guns (one had been damaged and hauled away earlier) and a handful of prisoners.

Even now the Federal defenders would not give up. The 4th Maine and the 99th Pennsylvania regiments rallied in the valley of Plum Run for a counterattack, and charged up the slope to reoccupy the boulder-strewn crest of the Devil's Den (6). They held it for less than fifteen minutes as the waves of Confederates swept up and over the high ground driving the stubborn defenders northward. Two Georgia regiments charged into the gap between Devil's Den and the Round Tops, a patch of ground that soon earned the sobriquet The Slaughter Pen (7). There they were assailed by the 40th New York regiment sent by Birney to reinforce Ward's collapsing line. The soldiers on both sides fought hand to hand in the valley of Plum Run, but eventually the 40th New York was forced to withdraw along with the rest of Ward's shattered command, and the Confederates were left in sole possession of the Devil's Den.

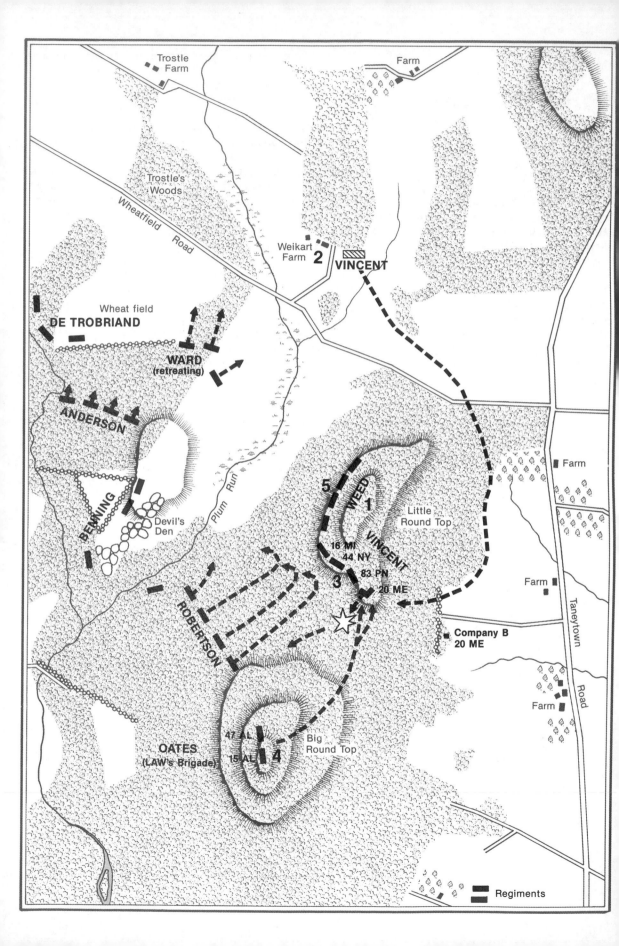

Trostle
Farm

Farm

Trostle's
Woods

Wheatfield Road

Weikart
Farm **2**

VINCENT

Wheat field

DE TROBRIAND

WARD
(retreating)

ANDERSON

BENNING

Devil's
Den

Plum Run

5

WEED

1

Little
Round Top

16 MI

VINCENT

44 NY

83 PN

3

20 ME

Farm

Farm

ROBERTSON

Company B
20 ME

Farm

47 AL

OATES
(LAW's Brigade)

15 AL

4

Big
Round Top

Taneytown Road

Farm

▬ Regiments

MAP 13

Little Round Top

4:30 - 6:00 p.m.

A few minutes before 4:00, while Meade was berating Sickles for having moved his corps, and Hood was pleading with Longstreet for permission to swing wider to the right, Federal Major General Gouverneur Warren of Meade's staff was riding up to the crest of Little Round Top (1). Warren saw at once that Little Round Top was the key to the whole Federal position, and he was alarmed to find it virtually unoccupied but for a small signal team. He sent several messengers off to seek reinforcements. One of them, Lt. Ranald Mackenzie, rode to Sickles' headquarters where he was told that Sickles could spare no troops. He then rode to Major General George Sykes, commander of the Fifth Corps, whose men were just arriving on the field. Sykes agreed to help, and sent a courier off to find to Major General James Barnes, his First Division commander, with orders to send a brigade to Little Round Top.

Sykes' courier instead found Brigadier General Strong Vincent near the Weikart Farm (2). Where was General Barnes? the messenger asked. Vincent answered with a question: "What are your orders?" The courier told him that General Sykes wanted a brigade sent to Little Round Top, and Vincent took it upon himself to accept the orders. "I will take the responsibility," Vincent replied, and he ordered his four regiments to march to the hill.

Believing that the northern face of Little Round Top was too steep, Vincent took his four regiments around the eastern side of the hill and climbed up into the swale between the Round Tops. There he found a shelf, or ledge, of rocky ground that has ever since been known as Vincent's Spur (3), and on it he placed his brigade facing southeast. He entrusted the left flank of this line to the 20th Maine regiment commanded by Colonel Joshua Chamberlain. The 386 officers and men of the 20th Maine constituted the extreme left flank of the entire Federal position that stretched all the way to Culp's Hill a mile to the north, and Vincent told Chamberlain that he must hold his position at all costs.

As the 20th Maine settled into place, the men of the 15th and 47th Alabama regiments of Evander

Law's Brigade were cresting the top of Big Round Top (4). The men of these regiments had marched 24 miles from New Guilford, Pennsylvania the night before, then hiked the long roundabout route along Willoughby Run to their attack positions, and finally had climbed the steep and difficult slope to the top of Big Round Top, all in near ninety degree heat, and without water. They had not yet fired a shot and they were already near exhaustion. Nevertheless, prodded to action by a staff officer, their commander, Colonel William C. Oates, ordered them forward, down the slope of Big Round Top into the swale of ground between the two hills. There, joined by three other regiments, they prepared to assault Little Round Top.

On their left and center, the Confederates made little progress. General Warren had sent Brigadier General Stephen H. Weed's Brigade to join Vincent's and secure the crest of Little Round Top (5). On the right, however, Oates' two regiments still outnumbered Chamberlain's 20th Maine, and Oates knew that if he could break through, or get around the flank, the whole line would dissolve. Despite their thirst and exhaustion, the Alabamians responded to Oates' call to battle, and they surged up the slope.

Four times the Alabamians attacked. Four times they were driven back. The men of the 20th Maine fired as fast as they could load. The combat was so close that men struggled hand to hand for the staff of the regimental colors. Acrid smoke filled the swale stinging the eyes of the participants, and parching the throats of the thirsty Alabamians. The Federals were hard pressed, but they did not break. Chamberlain pulled back his left to prevent being enveloped, and the down easters fought on.

Soon, however, the Federals began to run low on ammunition. As Chamberlain watched the Confederates gathering for what he assumed would be a fifth assault, he considered it unlikely that his men could withstand another attack without ammunition. Yet he could not give up his position. He could not defend, he could not retreat, and there was only one other alternative. "Fix bayonets!" he called. To the astonishment of the exhausted Alabama troops, the men of the 20th Maine spilled over the top of their rocky cover and charged downhill, their bayonets leveled. It was more than tired men could bear. The Alabamians fled, or too tired to flee, they surrendered. In a few moments the men of the 20th Maine stood panting at the bottom on the swale of ground between the Round Tops. The enemy was gone. The Federal left had held.

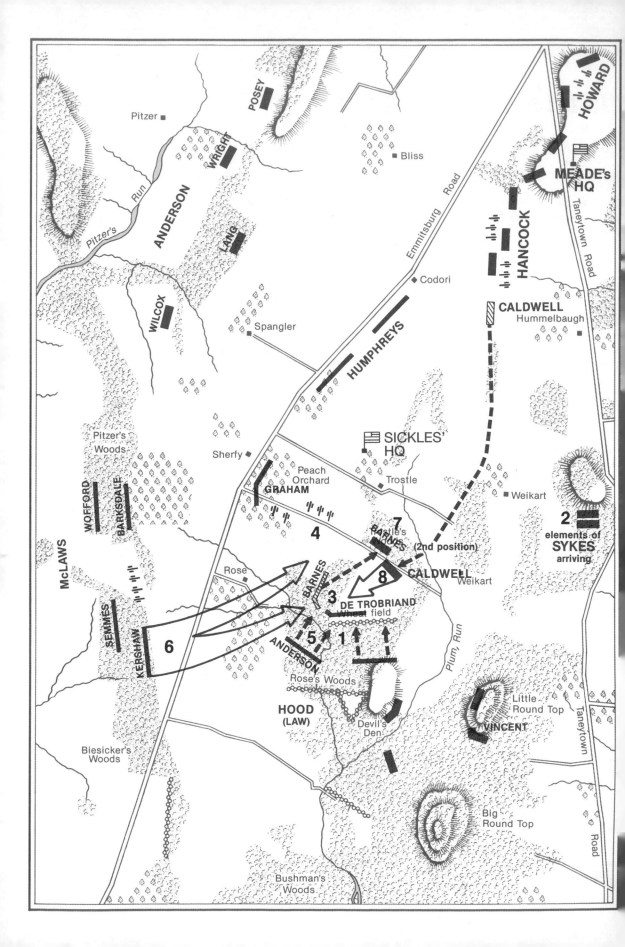

MAP 14

The Wheat Field

5:00 - 6:00 p.m.

Though Little Round Top remained secure, the Federals occupying its commanding height could take little satisfaction from what they could see unfolding in the fields and woods below them. The Confederates not only held the Devil's Den, from which their sharpshooters now sniped away at the Federals on Little Round Top, but the shrill yells and the smoke of their advancing line indicated that they were also driving northward against outnumbered Federals in Rose's Woods (1). The target of this renewed Confederate assault was the brigade of Brigadier General Regis de Trobriand, a Frenchman in the Union service. De Trobriand had started the day with about 1,800 men in five regiments, but he had sent two regiments to help Ward in the fight for Devil's Den; now his three remaining regiments faced an onslaught from two Confederate brigades.

The Federal defense of Rose's Woods and the adjoining wheat field was characterized by a desperate effort to rush reinforcements to Sickles' collapsing line. The first to arrive were from George Sykes' Fifth Corps (2). The First Division of this corps was commanded by Major General James Barnes who had three brigades at his disposal. Strong Vincent had already taken one of them to Little Round Top (see MAP #13), now Barnes ordered the other two to support de Trobriand in Rose's Woods. The Federals took up positions behind Plum Run on a rocky hill strewn with small boulders (3). De Trobriand's men held the left, with the 17th Maine taking position behind a stone wall bounding the southern edge of a wheat field. Barnes' men held the center and right, along the higher ground behind Plum Run Creek, then bending sharply to north to angle back toward the Wheatfield Road. There was a gap between the right wing of this position and the Federals in the Peach Orchard, but that gap was filled by several Federal batteries located along the Wheatfield Road (4).

The first Confederates to assail this Federal position belonged to the five Georgia regiments of Brigadier General George "Tige" Anderson's brigade (5). Taking advantage of the tree cover in Rose's Woods, the rebels advanced to the banks of Plum Run, then splashed across with a yell. The Federals more than held their own in this fight until 6:00 p.m. when McLaws unleashed J. B. Kershaw's brigade which came into the fight on Anderson's left (6). The Federal artillery along the Wheatfield Road tore great holes in the ranks of Kershaw's South Carolinians as they advanced. But though they took heavy loses, they did not flinch. For several minutes that seemed like hours, the fighting was at close quarters. Then Barnes ordered his two brigades to fall back. Though Sickles later criticized Barnes's decision, and even implied a lack of personal fortitude on his part, the Federals were being assailed on two sides and were all but surrounded. Barnes withdrew north of Wheatfield Road to Trostle's Woods (7) and with his withdrawal de Trobriand's men had to give way too. The Confederates pursued them into the wheat field.

On July 2, the wheat in George Weikart's wheat field was ripe, golden, and ready for harvest. At least one Georgian was so impressed by the quality of the wheat, that he gathered up some kernals to plant on his farm back home. But the Confederates had little time for such idylls, for they were only about half way across the field when they met a furious counterattack by the men of John C. Caldwell's Federal Division (8). Caldwell's men were from Hancock's Second Corps. Ordered to Sickles' aid, they had marched southward along the crest of Cemetery Ridge and now they pitched into the fight stepping literally over the top of Barnes' men, who were lying prone in Trostle's Woods. In the center of their line was the green flag of Brigadier General Patrick Kelly's Irish Brigade recruited from the boroughs of New York City. Caldwell drove his three brigades forward: across the wheat field, through Rose's Woods, and over Plum Run.

Caldwell's valiant charge recaptured the wheat field and regained the initiative, but his advance was too impetuous. In the process of rushing reinforcements to the front, Federal units had become intermingled. The three Federal divisions now fighting against Hood's Confederate division were from three different corps. Ostensibly, Sickles commanded the battlefield, but Barnes reported to Sykes, and Caldwell to Hancock. Worse, Sickles himself had fallen wounded and was no longer exercising command. In fact, no Federal officer was exercising effective overall command on this portion of the field. The lack of guiding authority meant that as Caldwell's men charged bravely forward, they were rushing into a trap.

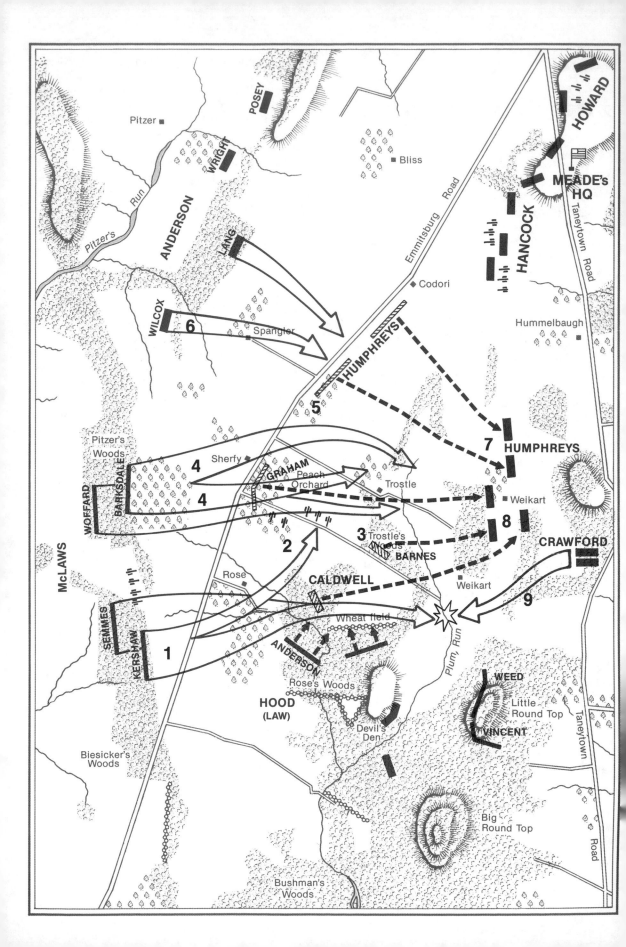

MAP 15

The Peach Orchard

6:00 - 7:30 p.m.

The Confederate assaults on Little Round Top, Devil's Den, and the Wheat Field had been carried out by the men of Hood's Division. All that time, the men of McLaws' Division stood waiting on their arms in the shade of Biesecker's and Pitzer's Woods. The original plan called for them to attack up the Emmitsburg Road after Hood had cleared the woods to the right. But the presence of Birney's Federal Division in those woods, and the fierceness of the resistance, meant that McLaws' men now had to come into the fight as a reinforcement for Hood. At six o'clock, Longstreet unleashed them.

The first to attack were the five and a half South Carolina regiments of J. B. Kershaw's Brigade (1). At 6:00, they stepped out of Biesecker's Woods, dressed ranks, and marched resolutely forward across the Emmitsburg Road, past the Rose House, and into the portion of Rose's Woods west of the Wheat Field. As they advanced, the Federal gunners along the Wheatfield Road fired canister into their packed ranks, doing horrible damage. Three of Kershaw's regiments veered toward the guns hoping to capture them (2); the three right hand regiments plunged into Rose's Woods on Anderson's left. It was this attack that convinced Barnes to order his two Federal brigades to fall back out of Rose's Woods across the Wheatfield Road to Trostle's Woods (3). Soon afterward, Caldwell's Division charged into the melee (see MAP #14).

Meanwhile, on Kershaw's left, the four Mississippi regiments of William Barksdale's Brigade advanced as well (4). For reasons that are not clear, their attack was delayed by some minutes. It was galling to Barksdale to watch Kershaw's men being raked by the Federal batteries along the Wheatfield Road, and he begged Longstreet to let him go forward. Longstreet replied: "Wait a little, we are all going in presently." At perhaps 6:15 Barksdale's men advanced. Their target was the Peach Orchard, the point of Sickles' salient, defended by four Pennsylvania regiments of Charles K. Graham's Brigade. Graham's men might have held their own against Barksdale's Mississippians, but Kershaw's Georgians were assailing them from the left at the same moment, and behind Barksdale was W. T. Wofford's Brigade. Outnumbered and attacked on two sides at once, Graham's men had no chance. Graham himself fell wounded, and the Federals began to fall back, slowly at first, then faster as the Confederates pressed their advantage.

The collapse of the Federal position in the Peach Orchard not only cut off the men of Caldwell's Division in Rose's Woods, but also uncovered the left flank of A. A. Humphreys' Division along the Emmitsburg Road (5). Now at last Longstreet's attack had the opportunity to roll up the Union line along the Emmitsburg Road as Lee had originally envisioned it. At about 6:30, as Barksdale's Mississippians assailed Humphreys' Division from the south, Wilcox's five Alabama regiments attacked frontally across the Emmitsburg Road (6). Humphreys sent to Sickles' headquarters for orders, but Sickles had fallen wounded and Birney had assumed command. He first ordered Humphreys to refuse his left to stop the onslaught of Barksdale's Brigade, then a few minutes later, he ordered Humphreys to fall back with his whole division to Cemetery Ridge.

That was easier said than done. Assailed on both front and flank, troops who were ordered to fall back could easily lose cohesion and begin to panic. But Humphreys kept his men under iron discipline. The noise of battle was so great that orders had to be shouted into the ears of company commanders. Federal regiments fired a volley, walked backward while re-loading, then stopped to fire again, repreating the process twenty times until they had fallen back a half mile to the crest of Cemetery Ridge (7). Though Humphreys lost 1,500 men out of his complement of 4,000, his patient withdrawal may have saved the Union army from disaster.

Meanwhile south of the Wheatfield Road, Caldwell's Division, too, was falling back, though much more precipitously. The victorious Confederates pursued the Federals to the banks of Plum Run where the Federals managed to form a new line (8). There they were bolstered by a gallant counterattack by the men of Samuel W. Crawford's Division of Sykes' Corps (9). After their long advance, the Confederates were not only exhausted, but their original formations had dissolved. They halted and began to fall back. In the act of trying to rally his men, Barksdale fell mortally wounded. By now it was dark and the fight for the Federal left sputtered to an end.

But despite the growing darkness, Lee had one more card to play.

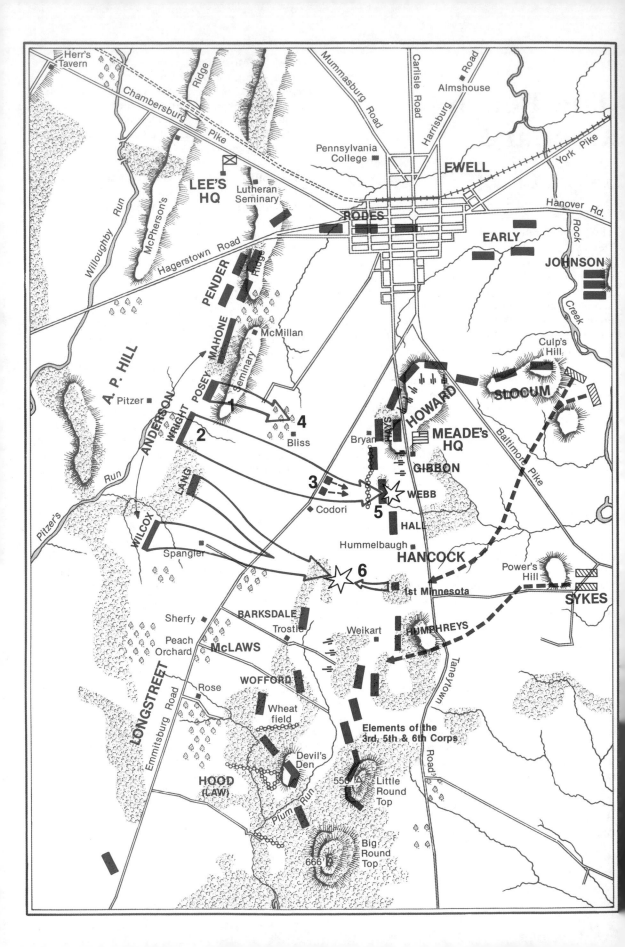

MAP 16

Cemetery Ridge

7:00 - 8:00 p.m.

The sun set at 7:30, but in the long twilight dusk of a midsummer's day, there was still plenty of light despite the clouds of smoke drifting about the battlefield. Watching the progress of the battle from his position on Seminary Ridge (1), Robert E. Lee witnessed the triumphal advance of Barksdale's Brigade as well as Wilcox's attack on the center of the Federal line. He watched the men of Humphreys' Division conduct their fighting retreat back to Cemetery Hill. The outcome of the battle, and perhaps the war, seemed to balance on a knife's edge. He instructed A. P. Hill to send the rest of Richard Anderson's Division forward to drive a wedge between the two halves of the Federal army.

Three of Anderson's brigades so far had taken no part in the afternoon's fight. From right to left they were A. R. Wright's Georgia Brigade, Carnot Posey's Mississippi Brigade, and William Mahone's Virginia Brigade. Wright's Georgians were posted in a line of trees on Seminary Ridge near where the equestrian statue of Lee now stands (2). From there they looked across a mile-wide stretch of open field toward Cemetery Ridge. Receiving the order to advance, they stepped out of the treeline and marched at a quickstep toward a fold in the ground where they would be protected from the Federal artillery on Cemetery Hill. There they paused briefly before charging ahead across the Emmitsburg Road and up onto Cemetery Ridge.

Earlier that afternoon, Hancock had adjusted his line to accomodate Sickles' advance to the Emmitsburg Road by sending two of his regiments out to the road to cover Humphreys' left (3). Those regiments now became the target of Wright's attack. With Humphrey's withdrawal, they consituted a lonely salient in front of the Federal line, and they were soon overwhelmed. Wright's Georgians drove them up the slope. Fully supported and pressed home, this attack might have been decisive, but on Wright's left the brigade of Carnot Posey was disorganized, and only two of his regiments advanced. Others deployed as skirmishers, and some did not move beyond the Bliss farm (4). Worse, due to a misunderstanding, William Mahone's Brigade, the largest and strongest in Anderson's Division, did not advance at all despite repeated urging by Anderson to do so.

Wright's Georgians pressed on alone. They reached the low stone wall atop Cemetery ridge and fought hand to hand with the soldiers of Gibbon's Second Corps among the guns of the Federal batteries (5). They had gained a precarious foothold on top of the ridge, but they could not stay there without support.

Just south of where Wright's Georgians and Webb's Pennsylvanians struggled, the Federal line was in complete disorder. For almost half a mile south of Hancock's position, the ridge was virtually undefended but for a few refugees from Sickles' shattered Corps and one lone regiment from the Second Corps: the 1st Minnesota commanded by William Colvill. Returning from helping direct a counterattack against Barksdale's Brigade, Hancock came upon the scene and took it all in at a glance: the half dozen Confederate regiments only 150 yards to the west in the valley of Plum Run, the lone Minnesota regiment on the crest, and behind it the disorganized Federal rear area. "My God!" he called out to no one in particular. "Are these all the men we have here?" Hancock calculated that something had to be done at once to buy time so that forces could be found to plug the hole. He turned to Colvill and gave him his orders. Pointing to the cluster of Confederate colors in the center of Wilcox's line he ordered: "Advance Colonel, and take those colors."

It was literally a forlorn hope, but Colvill responded at once. He ordered his men to throw off their packs and advance at the double quick. For a hundred yards they jogged forward into a hailstorm of bullets with men falling at every step (6). Then, with fifty yards to go, Colvill called upon his men to charge and, with a shout, they broke into a run. At the edge of Plum Run, mere feet from the enemy line, they halted and fired a volley. The shock of their charge threw Wilcox's men temporarily into confusion; instinctively they withdrew into the treeline or took cover to fire back. As the firing became general, the men of the 1st Minnesota retired hastily back to Cemetery Ridge. Of the 262 who made the charge, 215, including Colvill, failed to return. Only 47 survivors gathered at the top of the ridge, but the impetus of Wilcox's advance was halted.

To the north, Wright's Georgians gave up their foothold on Cemetery Ridge and fell back. From Little Round Top to Cemetery Hill, as twilight gave way to full darkness, the Federal line remained intact.

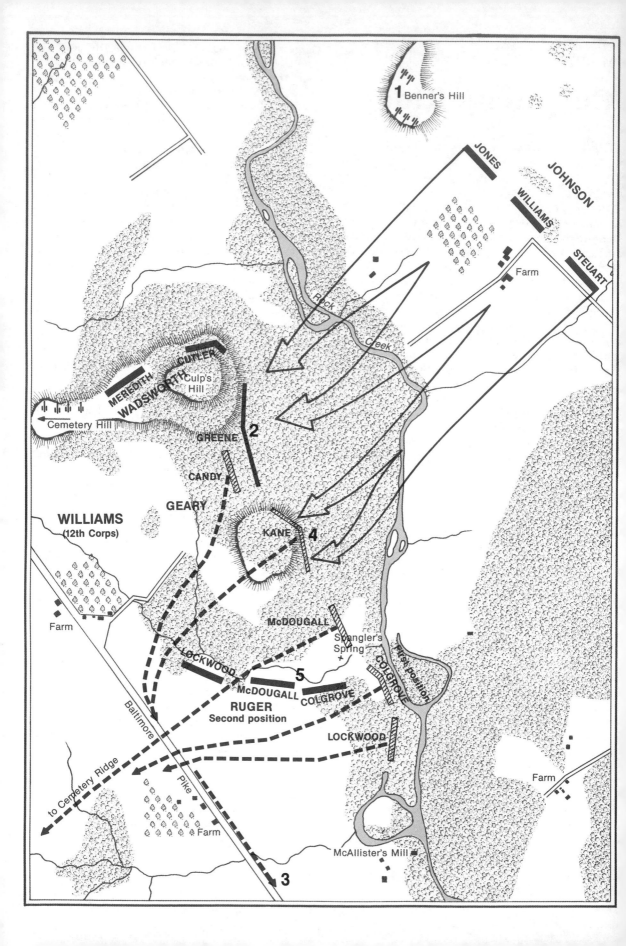

1 Benner's Hill

JOHNSON

JONES

WILLIAMS

STEUART

Farm

Rock

Creek

CUTLER

MEREDITH

WADSWORTH

Culp's Hill

Cemetery Hill

GREENE

2

CANDY

GEARY

WILLIAMS
(12th Corps)

KANE

4

McDOUGALL

Spangler's Spring

First position

LOCKWOOD

5

COLGROVE

Farm

McDOUGALL COLGROVE

RUGER
Second position

LOCKWOOD

Baltimore

to Cemetery Ridge

Pike

Farm

3

Farm

McAllister's Mill

MAP 17

Culp's Hill, I

7:30 - 10:30 p.m.

North and east of Cemetery Ridge, the three divisions of Dick Ewell's Corps—one third of the Confederate army—took no part in the afternoon fight. In Lee's scheme, Ewell was to provide a diversion to prevent the Federals from sending reinforcements to their embattled left. Of course, if an opportunity presented itself, Ewell was free to turn his diversion into a genuine attack, and Lee gave Ewell the discretionary authority to determine when and if he should do so.

At 4:00 p.m. as Hood's infantry stepped out of Biesecker's Woods to assail the Devil's Den and Little Round Top, Ewell's artillery on Benner's Hill (1) opened an artillery barrage on Slocum's Twelfth Corps on Culp's Hill and on Howard's Eleventh Corps on Cemetery Hill. But Ewell's barrage was not followed immediately by an infantry assault, and when at about 6:30 Sickles' Corps began to break apart under the pressure of Longstreet's attack, Meade ordered Slocum to send help in spite of the threat from Ewell.

Slocum had responsibility for the whole Federal right wing and he had turned the Twelfth Corps over to Alpheus Williams. The Twelfth was one of the smaller corps in the army, boasting only two divisions—those of Thomas H. Ruger and John Geary. Responding to Sickles' call for help, Ruger's Division marched off intact, leaving a gaping hole on the Federal right. Williams expected that Geary's division would slide to the right to fill the gap, but Slocum also ordered two of Geary's three brigades to follow Ruger, leaving only the 1,400 men of George Greene's Third Brigade (2), thinly stretched, to hold the heights. On Greene's left was the battered but still defiant division of James Wadsworth that had fought so well on McPherson's Ridge, but on his right the trenches formerly occupied by Ruger's Division stood empty. Ironically, neither Ruger nor Geary reached their new positions in time to make a difference in the fight against Longstreet. Geary's two brigades actually missed the turn to Cemetery Hill and marched off down the Baltimore Pike and out of the battle altogether (3).

At about the time that Meade pulled Ruger and Geary out of line on Culp's Hill, Ewell decided that with Longstreet's battle fully joined (he could hear the sounds of the fight from his headquarters), it was a propitious time to launch an attack of his own. His timing was certainly fortuitous, but his execution was badly flawed. For one thing, he never fully coordinated the efforts of his three divisions. The battle plan that Ewell suggested to his division commanders was that Johnson should attack the eastern slope of Culp's Hill with his entire division, and when fully engaged, Early would assail the saddle between Culp's Hill and Cemetery Hill. What role, if any, the division of Robert Rodes would play is uncertain. Still, such a plan had great promise, for as fate would have it, Johnson's men would advance directly against the empty Federal trenches abandoned by Ruger's Division.

Johnson did not begin his attack until sundown, and he was delayed by the difficult ground around Rock Creek. By the time his men began to ascend the thickly-forrested Culp's Hill, night had fallen. In the dark, amidst broken terrain, with Federal sharpshooters active in the trees, the Confederate advance slowed to a crawl. Meanwhile Greene sent urgent requests for support, and in response, Wadsworth sent him two regiments and Howard sent four more. With their help, and aided by the strength of the terrain, Greene managed to beat off Johnson's rather tentative assault. Eventually, however, the attackers discovered that the Federal lines on the extreme right were empty, and they scrambled into them (4). Greene refused his right, turning the Federal position on Culp's Hill into a bastion, and he anxiously called for Ruger's return. Williams was mortified that the enemy had taken his evacuated position, and he ordered Ruger to countermarch his division and take up a position just south of Culp's Hill (5) near Spangler's Spring where he could flank any Confederates on the hill once daylight returned.

Meanwhile, as Johnson's men crawled slowly up Culp's Hill, 3,500 men of Early's Division attacked Howard's Corps on Cemetery Hill (not shown). Hoke's Brigade, led on this occasion by Isaac Avery, struck Adelbert Ames' Federal Division on the northeast face of Cemetery Hill and drove it from its trenches. The rebels charged onto the broad crown of Cemetery Hill and struggled hand-to-hand with the Federal gunners who refused to abandon their guns and swung their ramrods like quarterstaffs. The gunners held on long enough for Hancock to rush part of Samuel S. Carroll's Brigade to the scene and drive back the attackers. In full darkness and unsupported, the Confederates gave way. By 10:30 it was over. Due largely to a lack of coordination, the Confederates had failed to seize Cemetery Hill though they retained their foothold on Culp's Hill.

THE THIRD DAY

July 3, 1863

After more than six hours of fighting, the relative silence of the battlefield after 10:30 seemed incongruous. With the guns silent, the quiet moans and plaintive calls of the wounded on both sides could be heard. A full moon that rose at 10:00 cast a pale silver glow over the grisly fields where the bodies of more than 15,000 men lay scattered. Some lay in neat rows where they had fallen, cut down by a blast of cannister or a well-aimed volley of rifle fire; others were locked in the contorted postures of those for whom death had come more slowly. Many who lived still, called out quietly for the aid of friends, or for anyone who would bring them water. Others waited patiently and stoically in field hospitals for the surgeon's knife to take an arm or a leg.

Of the 15,000 who had fallen, three fifths of them wore blue, for despite being on the defensive, the Federals had lost nearly 9,000 men on July 2 as compared to Confederate losses of some 6,000. Sickles' Corps had virtually ceased to exist; other units, such as Cald-

Brigadier General Lewis Armistead, his hat on his sword point, leads Confederate forces into "the Angle" at the climax of Pickett's Charge. Within moments Armistead fell mortally wounded among the guns of Cushing's Battery. According to tradition, his last words were for his old friend, Win Hancock, who commanded that portion of the Union line. (National Archives)

well's Division of Hancock's Corps, had been so badly mauled they could not be relied upon to fight again soon. The ground that Sickles had thought so good had been lost as well, and Confederate soldiers occupied Devil's Den, the Wheatfield, and the high ground around the Peach Orchard. It had been a disastrous day for the Federal cause.

On the other hand, the Federals still clung to Cemetery Hill, the Round Tops, and to the modest ridge that connected them. The Union army's position stretched in an unbroken line from Big Round Top, which the 20th Maine occupied after dark, across the front of Little Round Top, along Cemetery Ridge to Cemetery Hill, and then curled around the northern slope of Cemetery Hill to Culp's Hill. If anything, the loss of Sickles' salient had helped the Federals consolidate their line which now resembled the famous "fish hook" configuration. Even more importantly, the rest of the Federal army had at last arrived. Even with the losses of the last two days, Meade could put some 56,000 soldiers into the line. The Army of the Potomac was unified, strongly placed, and ready for anything that Lee could throw at it. Perhaps it had not been so disastrous a day after all.

At 11:00 Meade met with his corps commanders at his head- quarters. A dozen generals crowded into the tiny room, no larger than ten by twelve feet. In the weak yellow light of

Union corps commanders crowd into Meade's tiny headquarters behind Cemetery Ridge on the evening of July 2. Though Meade had already decided to stay and fight, he polled his senior officers for their opinions. They voted to stay and fight. (Library of Congress)

camp lanterns, Meade invited their views on the day's fight. After a lengthy discussion, Meade's chief of staff, Major General Dan Butterfield, posed the crucial question: Should the army stay and fight it out in its present position, or decamp under the cover of darkness and head south down the Baltimore Pike. Meade told his officers that he would be bound by their decision, and at least a few claimed afterward that Meade's tone suggested that he was not eager to stay and face another such day. In fact, however, Meade had already wired Halleck: "I shall remain in my present position tomorrow." Since he had sent that message, however, the rebels had gained a foothold on Culp's Hill and assailed Cemetery Hill, and perhaps Meade sought confirmation of his decision. If so, it was no doubt satisfying that his corps commanders voted unanimously to stay and fight. "Such then is the decision," Meade said quietly, and he dismissed the meeting. At midnight the corps commanders returned to their commands to await the dawn, now less than five hours away.

On their side of the field, the Confederates could take justifiable pride in the day's accomplishments, for they had fought splendidly. They had engaged forces double their own number and driven them from strong positions while inflicting heavy losses. But they had not achieved a decisive breakthrough, and just what exactly they had won besides a few acres of blood-soaked ground was unclear. Of course they were tantalized by all the might-have-beens. Only by the narrowest of margins had the 20th Maine clung to Little Round Top.

Winfield Scott Hancock poses at the center of a group of Union officers, all of whom played important roles at Gettysburg. Left to right they are Francis Barlow, wounded in the first day's fight; David Birney, who commanded in the Wheat Field on the second day; and John Gibbon, whose division manned the line in front of the clump of trees on the third day. (National Archives)

George Pickett was eager as a puppy to embark on the charge that bears his name. But afterward he was resentful, and for the rest of his life he blamed Lee for ruining his division. (National Archives)

Wright's Brigade of Anderson's Division had pierced through the Federal line on Cemetery Ridge, and Avery's Brigade of Early's Division had done the same on Cemetery Hill, and in both cases had been forced to fall back because of a lack of support. If only Posey and Mahone had advanced with Wright! If only Rodes had supported Early! If only there had been more daylight left! If only Pickett had been present with his division! Such siren songs played on the mind of more than one gray clad officer that night, as they have played on the minds of historians since. But the man whose opinion mattered was Lee. What was he thinking that night?

Having committed himself to a fight at Gettysburg, and come so close, Lee believed that he could not withdraw now without admitting defeat. And defeat in this battle meant defeat in the campaign. Such magnificent soldiers! If they could achieve so much in assaults that were indifferently coordinated, surely a concentrated and coordinated assault against a weak point in the Union line would settle the issue. If Wright's lone brigade had managed to crest Cemetery Ridge unsupported, what might a dozen brigades do? Moreover, perhaps the means were at hand. Longstreet's Third Division, that of George Pickett with its fifteen fresh regiments of Virginia troops, had arrived late in the afternoon on July 2 while the fight was still in progress. Pickett had told Lee that despite their long march, his men were ready to go straight into the fight, but Lee had stayed

Alfred Waud's drawing of Pickett's Charge seen from behind Union lines. The artist's perspective is that of one standing near the clump of trees. (Library of Congress)

him. "I will have important work for you to-morrow," Lee said. So while his men rested, Pickett had watched from Seminary Ridge as Wright's Georgians pierced the enemy line, and then fell back again.

Another Confederate officer had arrived on Seminary Ridge that afternoon. Dusty and saddle sore, J. E. B. Stuart rode up to Lee's head-quarters tent well ahead of his cavalrymen just after noon. "Well, General Stuart," Lee re-marked, "you are here at last." Though hardly a stern censure, such a comment was so un-usual for Lee that Stuart felt the sting of im-plied rebuke. He tried to compensate for his tardiness by pointing out that he had brought with him over a hundred captured wagons, fully loaded. But Lee stopped such protesta-tions with a wave of his hand. As with Pickett,

Lee told Stuart to have his men rest that eve-ning, for he would need them the next day. Stuart left the tent disspirited, his shoulders slumped with more than fatigue, but there is no evidence that Lee had chastized him be-yond the implications of that "at last."

With Pickett's fresh troops to provide the spearhead, and Stuart's cavalry to conduct the pursuit, Lee believed that the next day his army would complete the job so magnificently begun. Before he slept, he sent a message to Ewell instructing him to renew his assault on Culp's Hill at dawn. Finally, at midnight, about the time that Meade dismissed his meeting of corps commanders, Lee lay down for four hours sleep. He would be up early; July 3 could be the day that determined the outcome of the war.

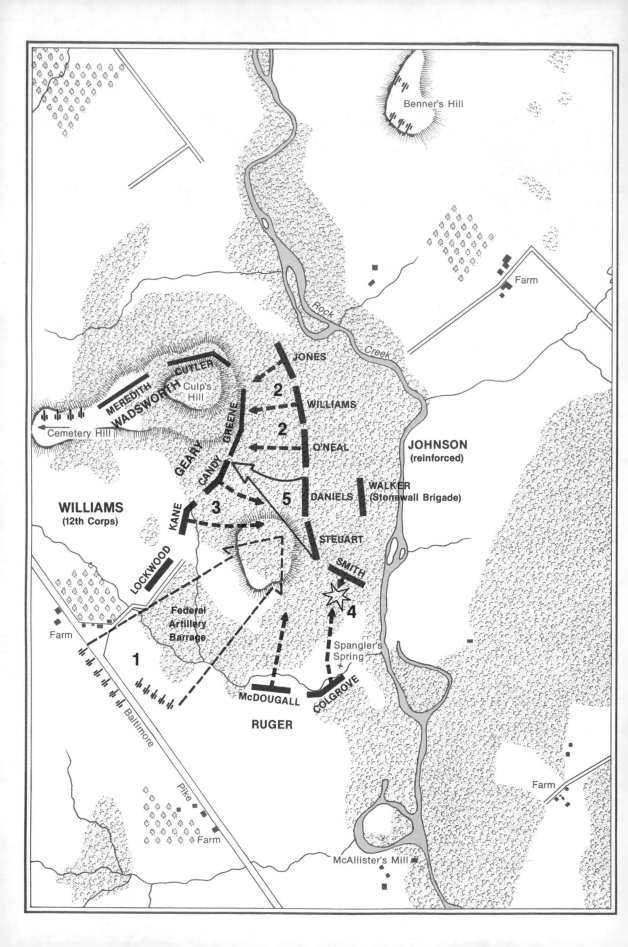

Benner's Hill

Farm

Rock Creek

JONES

CUTLER

MEREDITH

WADSWORTH

Culp's Hill

2

WILLIAMS

Cemetery Hill

2

O'NEAL

GREENE

GEARY

CANDY

JOHNSON
(reinforced)

WALKER
(Stonewall Brigade)

DANIELS

WILLIAMS
(12th Corps)

KANE

3

5

STEUART

LOCKWOOD

SMITH

Federal
Artillery
Barrage

4

1

Spangler's
Spring

Baltimore

McDOUGALL

COLGROVE

RUGER

Pike

Farm

Farm

Farm

McAllister's Mill

MAP 18

Culp's Hill, II

3:30 - 10:15 a.m.

The plan that Lee devised for the destruction of the Federal army was simple enough: He would attack both its left and right flanks simultaneously. Reinforced by Pickett's fresh division, Longstreet would renew his assault against the Federal left, while Ewell followed up on Johnson's late evening successes on Culp's Hill. Whether or not this plan could have achieved what Lee hoped for it is another Confederate might-have-been, for circumstances conspired to render it impracticable from the very start.

First of all, Lee's plan did not take into account Federal initiatives. Believing that the Federal army had been all but shattered on July 2, Lee did not think it was in any condition to launch an attack of its own. But Federal Major General Alpheus Williams, whose trenches Johnson's men had occupied the night before on Culp's Hill, was eager to get them back, and after he returned from the conference in Meade's headquarters after midnight, he spent most of the night preparing to do just that. He pulled back the flanks of both Geary's and Ruger's Divisions to open a clear field of fire for the Federal artillery (1), and at 3:30, a full hour before first light, 26 Union guns opened on Confederate positions on the southern slope of Culp's Hill. After an hour of this, Williams ordered two of Geary's brigades (those of Kane and Greene) to advance and reclaim the lost entrenchments.

But pursuant to Lee's orders, Johnson had been preparing to renew his own attack. Overnight Ewell had ordered two of Rodes' Brigades and one of Early's to march to Johnson's support so that when the Federal artillery barrage broke upon them, the Confederates on or near Culp's Hill had a total of seven brigades available. Thus Geary's assault was stillborn as the Confederates launched an attack of their own (2). Even though the Confederate superiority of numbers was minimized by the thick forrest and rocky terrain in the pre-dawn darkness, Geary soon felt compelled to send his third brigade into the fight (3), and he was much relieved soon afterward to welcome the first supports sent by Meade from Howard's and Hancock's Corps.

With the failure of the initial Confederate assault, the battle for Culp's Hill broke down into a series of small unit encounters with nearly continuous fire on both sides. Johnson probed for a weak spot, sending first one brigade, then another, toward different points of the Federal line. On the other side, the Federals, too, probed for a weak spot. Slocum, commanding the whole Federal right wing, ordered Silas Colgrove to send two regiments to attack what he presumed was the vulnerable Confederate flank. Colgrove thought the move ill-advised, but he obeyed the order and sent the 27th Indiana and the 2nd Massacusetts into a hornet's nest of fire from forces more than double their strength (4). The two regiments advanced gamely, and fought heroically, but after losing nearly half their number, they were forced back to their original positions.

At about 10:00 a.m. with the sun already high in the sky, Johnson decided it was time to risk the outcome of the fight on one all-out effort. He sent the brigades of George H. Steuart and Junius Daniel crashing into Geary's line near the crest of Culp's Hill (5). Raked by artillery fire on their left, and rifle fire to the front, they advanced gallantly, but with no better results than before. At 10:15, Johnson finally called off the fight. As his men began to fall back down the hill, Geary's charged out of their entrenchments in pursuit. By 11:00, the Federals had recovered their old lines on Culp's Hill, and the Federal "fishhook" line was re-established.

From a Confederate perspective, Johnson's repulse on Culp's Hill was all the more tragic because it had taken place while the rest of the battlefield remained quiet. Though Lee had conceived of Johnson's attack as one half of a double envelopment, Longstreet had failed to order Pickett's men to be ready to attack at dawn. Worse, on his own initiative Longstreet had ordered his other two divisions to begin a gradual eastward shift in anticipation of making a move around the Federal left, south of the Round Tops. When Lee came riding up to Longstreet's tent just after dawn, he was disappointed and even angered to find that Longstreet, both by omission and comission, had done so much to spoil his plan. At once, he sent word to Ewell that Longstreet was not ready to cooperate. Ewell received the memo at 5:00 a.m., but it was too late, Johnson was already engaged.

With the collapse of his original plan, Lee now had to re- think his battlefield strategy. One thing was clear, he was not about to adopt Longstreet's plan to disengage and move south. "The enemy is there," Lee told his Old War Horse, "and I am going to strike him."

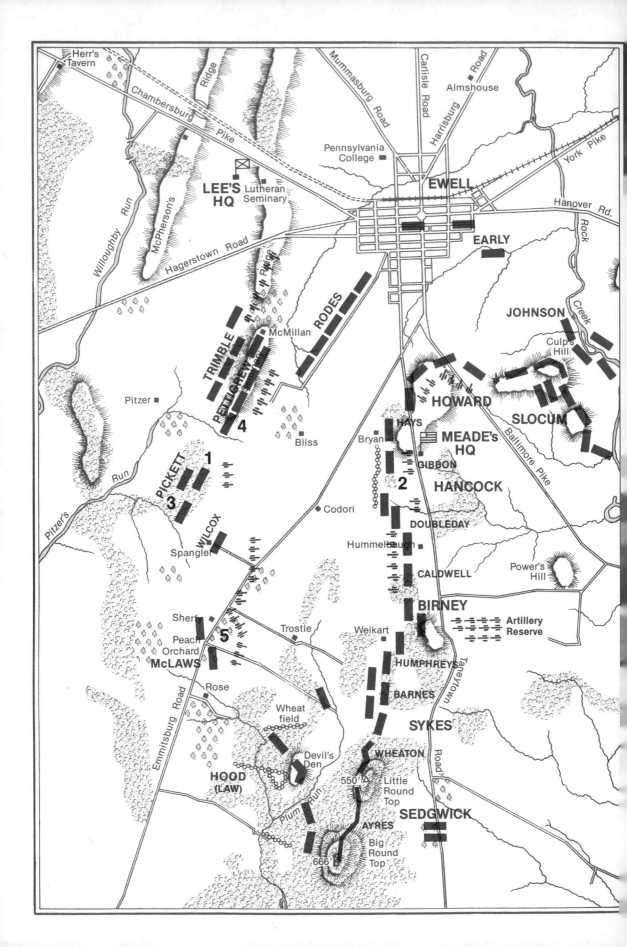

MAP 19

Planning the Grand Assault

11:00 a.m. - 3:00 p.m.

At midmorning Lee and Longstreet rode northward together along Seminary Ridge to a point of woods at nearly the center of the long Confederate line (1). There Lee examined the Federal position across the open fields that separated the two armies. He knew that Meade had been forced to send reinforcements to both of his flanks, and that those reinforcements presumably had come from the center. Perhaps here, where the Federals had little natural protection from thick woods or high hills, perhaps this was where they were most vulnerable. If he sent his magnificent infantry on a narrow front against a single point in that thin blue line, it could not fail to win through. Of course the men would be at risk while crossing those open fields, but that could be minimized by concentrating a massed artillery barrage on the Union line beforehand.

Lee noticed a small clump of trees, standing alone on the ridge line and easily recognizable because of its distinctive umbrella shape (2). If Longstreet's entire Corps, bolstered now by Pickett's fresh division, assailed the enemy all at once, guiding on that clump of trees, the pressure would be irresistable. Once over the ridgeline, the men could wheel right and left to come up behind the Federals on Cemetery Hill and Little Round Top. The whole Federal position would dissolve.

Lee turned to Longstreet to explain his plan. But Longstreet was immediately critical. The divisions of Hood and McLaws, he said, could not be removed from where they were on the Confederate right. Besides, they had fought hard yesterday and were tired. Lee accepted Longstreet's judgement about Hood and McLaws. But there was still Pickett, and Lee could patch together two relatively fresh divisions from A. P. Hill's Corps. The three divisions could be found. Longstreet remained skeptical. How many men would there be in the attack? he asked. About 15,000, Lee replied. According to Longstreet's own memoirs, he then told Lee:

> "General, I have been a soldier all my life. I have been with soldiers engaged in fights by couples, by squads, companies, regiments, divisions, and armies, and should know, as well as anyone, what soldiers can do. It is my opinion that no fifteen thousand men ever arrayed for battle can take that position."

They may not have been his exact words, but there is no doubt that Longstreet was frank, even blunt, in expressing his opposition to a frontal attack. He again proposed that the army move to the south and take up a blocking position between Gettysburg and Washington forcing Meade to assume the tactical offensive. But Lee believed that a frontal attack would work, and after hearing Longstreet out, he ordered him to make the necessary arrangements.

With a perceptible lack of enthusiasm, Longstreet set to work to organize the grand assault. Of course Pickett's fresh division of Virginians would form the spearhead (3). Heth's division, now commanded by Pettigrew since Heth was wounded, would form on Pickett's left (4). Two of Anderson's brigades and two of Dorsey Pender's, all under the command of Marylander Isaac Trimble, would form behind Pettigrew.

It took some time for all the units to march to their assigned positions, and meanwhile Colonel Edward Porter Alexander assembled the army's artillery so that it could focus its power on the center of the Federal line. From 11:00 a.m. when the firing on Culp's Hill finally died out, until 1:00 in the afternoon, a strange quiet descended on the battlefield while these preparations took place. Then at 1:00 the silence was broken by a single discharge from one of the Confederate cannons near the Peach Orchard (5)—a sharp aural slap in the thick air of mid day. It was followed by another. Then there was a pause, as if the very earth were drawing breath, and 150 Confederate guns began the most furious artillery barrage in the history of North America. Shot and shell rained down on Cemetery Ridge, and Federal gunners ran to their pieces to return fire. The valley quickly filled with smoke, and Federal infantry on the ridge hugged the earth. For two hours the barrage continued. Then, slowly, it died out.

Now it was the infantry's turn. Out of the tree line on Seminary Ridge stepped ten thousand armed men. Their regimental colors drooped lazily in the still air. The smoke covering the field rose slowly, almost like a curtain rising for the main event. Pickett spurred his horse up to Longstreet and, saluting smartly, reported that his division was formed and ready. Should he commence the charge? Longstreet found he could not speak the words. He merely nodded his head.

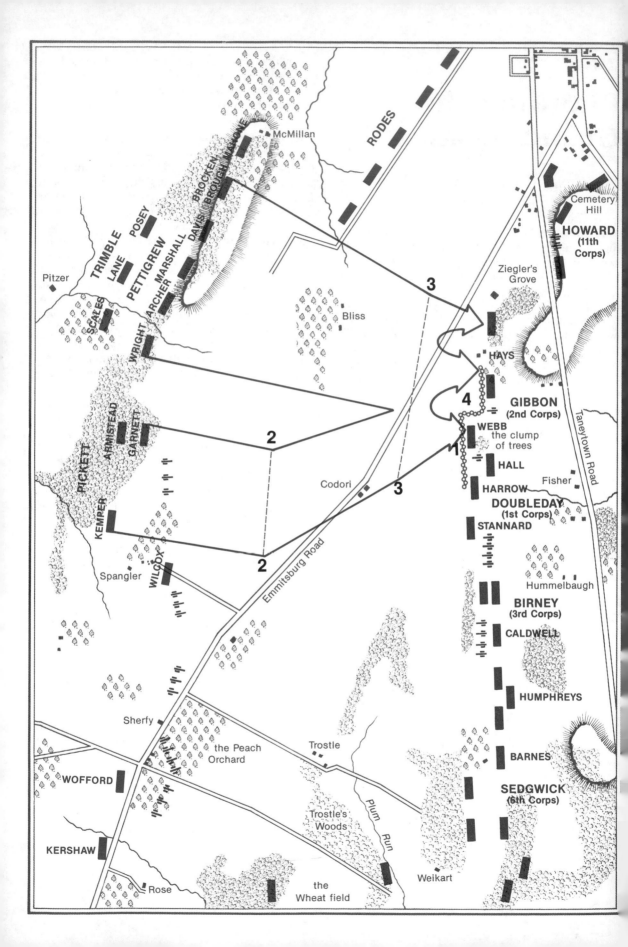

MAP 20

Pickett's Charge

3:00 - 3:30 p.m.

The soldiers who manned the Federal line on Cemetery Ridge nearest the clump of trees belonged to John Gibbon's Second Division of Hancock's Second Corps. They were from Massachusetts, Michigan, New York, Maine, and Pennsylvania. The remnant of the 1st Minnesota regiment, which had lost 82 percent of its men in a gallant sacrifice the day before, was there too. The center of Gibbon's position, in the very shade of the clump of trees, was occupied by three regiments of the Philadelphia Brigade commanded by Alexander Webb (1). Webb had been promoted to brigadier general only the day before; now he stood at the very epicenter of the war.

With the opening salvoes of the Confederate bombardment, Webb's men threw themselves to the ground or lay prone behind the low stone wall. Shells plowed up the earth, and shattered the stones, sending fragments flying in all directions, but because the Confederate gunners tended to fire high, most of the ordnance passed over the ridge and fell in the rear area killing artillery horses and wrecking caissons. The Federal artillerists returned fire, but with all the smoke it was difficult to tell if they fired to any advantage. After an hour, the Federal chief of artillery, Brigadier General Henry Hunt, ordered his gunners to slow their rate of fire. He did not want to be low on ammunition when the inevitable infantry assault took place. Soon afterward, the Confederates ceased firing, and the men of Webb's Brigade rose up slowly to look around. Through the clouds of rising smoke they could see the men of Pickett's and Pettigrew's divisions emerge from the dark treeline on Seminary Ridge. It was a sight none of them would ever forget: magnificent and terrible.

As a gentle westerly breeze blew the smoke away and sent the regimental colors billowing, the Confederates began to advance. They moved at a walking pace: one hundred yards to the minute. Since it was more than a mile across the open fields, it would take them sixteen minutes to cross it. Soon after they passed through the ranks of their own artillery and into the open fields, Federal artillery shells began to land within their ranks. The explod-

ing shells left gaps in their line, and a scattering of bodies in their wake. Confederate officers called for the men to "Close up!" The gaps filled, and the advance continued. Half way across, Pickett's Division executed a smart left oblique, as if on the parade ground, to close ranks with Pettigrew (2). Then several hundred yards further on, in the swale of a modest depression, the whole line stopped to realign its formation (3). Unbelieving, a Union soldier sputtered: "My God! They're dressing ranks." Arrayed now in a solid front, the attackers resumed their advance, crossing the Emmitsburg Road, and climbing over the rail fence at the foot of the slope. They were close enough to see the faces of their enemy, and the survivors quickened their pace as they began to ascend the ridge. Only yards away, they began to cheer, and they hit the Union line at a dead run.

A hundred yards north of the clump of trees, the low stone wall which the Federal soldiers were using for cover made a sharp ninety degree turn and ran eastward for eighty yards before continuing northward (4). At the angle in this wall, the men of the 71st Pennsylvania watched with a mixture of awe and terror as several thousand screaming men rushed toward their small section of the battlefront. Their nerves began to break, and several blue-coated soldiers fled from the wall seeking safety in the rear. Others followed, and then the whole regiment was in retreat, officers and men alike, running for their lives. The rebels came charging over the wall in pursuit. The high water mark of the Confederacy, at least in the minds of those soldiers of Armistead's and Garnett's brigades at the spearpoint of the Confederate charge, must have been that moment when the 71st Pennsylvania broke and fled. Surely they must have expected that in the next moment the rest of the Union line would crumble as well, and leave them masters of the field.

Such a vision of imminent victory inspired Confederate Brigadier General Lewis Armistead to seize the moment. His men must get through the breach and complete their work—and soon—lest they squander the opportunity. Dashing to the front he called out for his men to follow: "Come on, boys," he cried, raising his hat on his sword point, "Give them the cold steel! Who will follow me?" He leapt over the wall and ran forward into the breach in the Union line. Watching from Seminary Ridge, this was the moment of highest hope for the Confederate command. Even Longstreet thought that the attack might win through after all. But it was not to be.

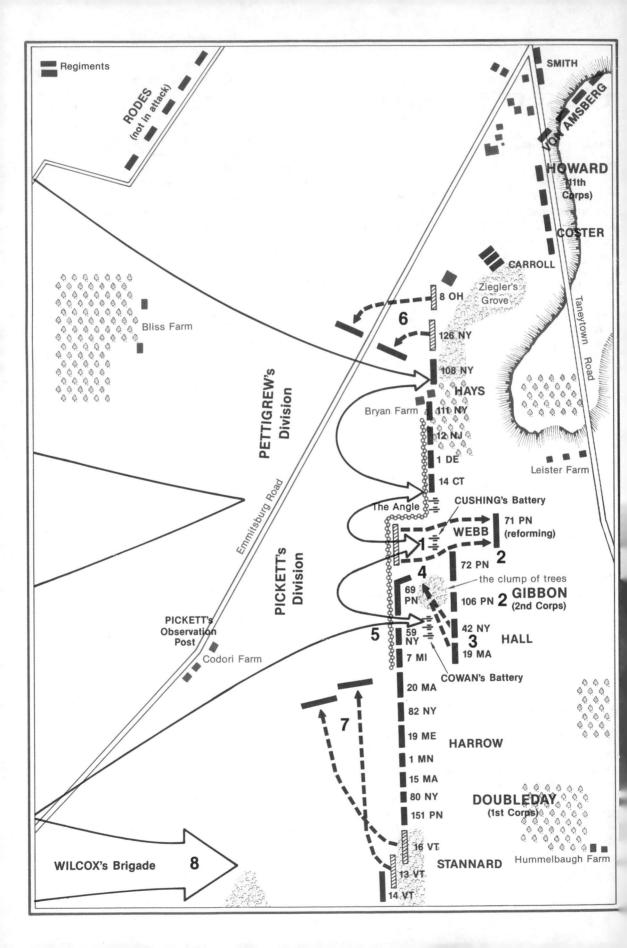

Regiments

RODES
(not in attack)

SMITH

VON AMSBERG

HOWARD
(11th Corps)

COSTER

CARROLL

Ziegler's Grove

8 OH

6

126 NY

Bliss Farm

108 NY

HAYS

Bryan Farm

111 NY

12 NJ

1 DE

14 CT

Leister Farm

Taneytown Road

The Angle

CUSHING's Battery

71 PN
(reforming)

WEBB

1

72 PN

2

PETTIGREW's Division

Emmitsburg Road

PICKETT's Division

the clump of trees

4

69 PN

106 PN

2

GIBBON
(2nd Corps)

59 NY

42 NY

3

HALL

5

7 MI

19 MA

PICKETT's Observation Post

Codori Farm

COWAN's Battery

20 MA

82 NY

7

19 ME

HARROW

1 MN

15 MA

80 NY

DOUBLEDAY
(1st Corps)

151 PN

16 VT

Hummelbaugh Farm

WILCOX's Brigade

8

13 VT

14 VT

STANNARD

MAP 21

The Angle

3:30 - 4:00 p.m.

Armistead's dash into the angle of the Union line at the head of several hundred Confederate soldiers was both fateful and poignant. Armistead had served in the "Old Army" with Winfield Scott Hancock. When he had resigned from the army to "go South," Hancock had given a dinner party in his honor, and they had parted with firm handclasps and mutual tears. Now Armistead led the charge on Hancock's Corps. Still shouting for his men to follow, he ran toward the battery of Lieutenant Alonzo Cushing twenty yards beyond the stone wall. Cushing had been mortally wounded, but clutching the wound in his stomach, he cried out, "Webb, I will give them one more shot!" He pulled the lanyard, sending a storm of cannister into the face of the attackers; then fell dead among his guns.

Within seconds, Armistead, too, was down, mortally wounded within a few feet of Cushing's body. Today a stone tablet marks the spot where he fell, and it has traditionally been accorded the distinction of being the high water mark of the Confederacy (1). Such a distinction is merited. With Armistead's fall the impetus of the Confederate charge was lost. Both Garnett and Kemper had fallen as well, so that now there was no living officer above the rank of colonel to guide the attack. The advantage of numbers at the point of attack still greatly favored the Confederates, but they were leaderless and directionless.

For their part, the Federal defenders benefited from timely and even inspired leadership. Webb plugged the gap in his line by ordering the 72nd and 106th Pennsylvania regiments to counter- attack (2). Gamely, they moved up the reverse slope and took the rebels under fire. Hancock ordered two other regiments (the 19th Massachusetts and the 42nd New York) into the melee around the clump of trees (3). On the attackers' right, the 69th Pennsylvania had held its position along the stone wall and fired into the rebels' flank (4).

The Confederates now faced an awkward moment. Psychologically, they had concentrated all of their effort on achieving their objective: reaching the enemy line and breaking it. They had done that, and yet Federal soldiers continued to return fire, not only from the front, but from both flanks. Though they had broken the Union line, they could not exploit the breakthrough without leadership and direction. One bold group of rebels—led by a major— launched themselves toward Cowan's Battery just south of the clump of trees (5). Cowan was nearly out of ammunition, but as the rebel infantry charged, he loaded his last round—double cannister—and fired. When the smoke cleared, the attacking infantry was gone.

North of the angle, Pettigrew's Division, with Trimble in support, was closing on the Federal division of Alexander Hays. With admirable courage, the Confederates pressed their attack despite terrible losses. Hays ordered two regiments (the 126th New York and the 8th Ohio) to swing out from the line and face southward so as to take the Confederates in their flank (6). Thinking similarly, Hancock ordered two Vermont regiments of George J. Stannard's Brigade of the First Corps to execute the same movement against Kemper's Brigade south of the angle (7).

A few minutes before 4:00, Webb finally succeeded in rallying the men of the 71st Pennsylvania and he brought them into line alongside the 72nd. He called on them to charge, but though they had come back into the fight and stood their ground manfully, they could not be persuaded to advance. Lieutenant Frank Haskell, aide to General Gibbon, tried to encourage the men by ordering their color bearer forward, hoping that his brave example would inspire the rest. It did, but not, perhaps, in the way Haskell expected. The color bearer went forward as ordered, but he did so alone, and met the inevitable fate as he was shot down. Seeing their flag fall, something snapped in the minds of the men of the two Pennsylvania regiments. With a shout, they surged forward.

Virtually leaderless, with enemy fire on both their flanks and advancing infantry to their front, the Confederates still inside the angle realized that the game was up. Those who could, fell back as fast as their pride would allow; others threw up their hands in surrender.

Several hundred yards to the south, the men of Wilcox's and Perry's Brigades, late in starting out, only now assailed the Federal line south of the angle (8). It was much too little too late. They, too, fell back, having achieved nothing. Watching all this from a position near the Codori House, Pickett turned his horse's head toward Seminary Ridge. The assault had failed.

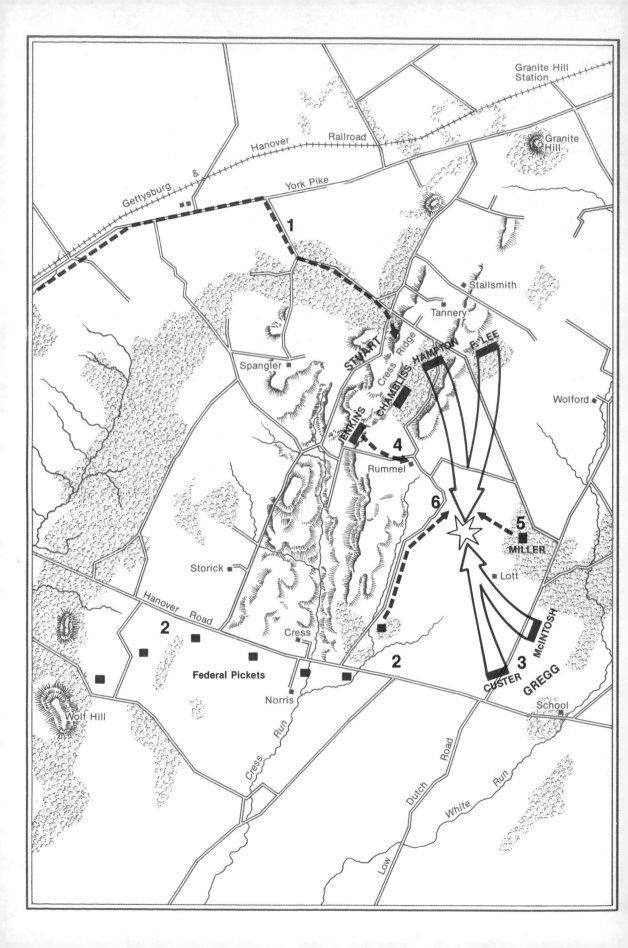

MAP 22

The Cavalry Action

3:30 - 5:00 p.m.

While Union and Confederate infantrymen struggled hand to hand on Cemetery Ridge, a similarly dramatic battle was being fought three miles to the east by the cavalry forces of each side. Chastened by Lee's obvious disappointment, and determined to win back his commander's favor, J.E.B. Stuart rode eastward out of Gettysburg on the morning of July 3 at the head of four cavalry brigades—five thousand men, fully four fifths of the army's mounted force. Stuart afterward declared that his job was only to guard the left of Ewell's Corps, but the size of his force, and his actions on the day, suggest that his mission was much more ambitious. It is likely that his object was nothing less than a mounted attack on the Federal rear, either in conjunction with Pickett's Charge, or as a follow up to the expected breakthrough.

At mid-morning, with firing still continuing on Culp's Hill, Stuart and his men rode out the York Pike well beyond the flank of both armies, then turned south onto a farm road (1) and ascended Cress's Ridge. From this vantage point, Stuart had a commanding view of the rolling farmland to the south. Two miles away he could make out the line of the Hanover Road, guarded only by Federal pickets (2). But with his field glasses, Stuart could also see that near the intersection of the Hanover Road and Low Dutch Road there was a large body of Yankee cavalry, at least two full brigades (3). They were the brigades of John B. McIntosh and young George Armstrong Custer, the latter only two years out of West Point and promoted from captain to brigadier general only days before. Both brigades were under the command of David McM. Gregg, one of the Union army's better cavalry commanders.

Stuart determined to lure the Federal cavalry into the open with a body of skirmishers, then fall upon them with his whole force. At 1:00 p.m., when the sound of the Confederate artillery bombardment of Cemetery Ridge reached his ears, he ordered the troopers of A. G. Jenkins' brigade to dismount and advance to the vicinity of the Rummel Farm (4). Soon afterward, mounted troopers from the brigades of Fitz Lee and Wade Hampton emerged from the treeline on Cress's Ridge and were seen by the Federals below. Stuart was angry, believing that their premature appearance had spoiled his plan. But Gregg was hardly surprised. Howard's lookouts on Cemetery Hill had spotted the rebel cavalry leaving Gettysburg that morning and had wig-wagged him the news. Nevertheless, the appearance of these forces led Gregg to turn to Custer with a request. Custer was under orders to return at once with his brigade to the Federal left, but Gregg asked him if he would stay. Always game for a fight, Custer told Gregg that he would stay if Gregg ordered him to do so. Though he lacked the authority, Gregg had a true leader's moral courage and assumed the responsibility.

By now dismounted skirmishers from both sides were sniping at each other near the Rummel Farm. Stuart sent three regiments in a galloping charge to drive the Federals off; Gregg responded by supporting his skirmishers with two regiments of his own. Deciding that the decisive moment had come, Stuart played his ace. He ordered all of Hampton's and Lee's cavalry—between 2,500 and 3,000 men—to charge. It was as dramatic in its way as the charge of Pickett's infantry. The rebel horsemen thundered down the gentle slope and across the open fields, the fastest in the forefront, losing formation as they rode. Gregg ordered Custer to counter-attack, and placing himself at the head of his brigade, the 22-year old general ordered his bugler to sound the charge.

From opposite sides of the open fields, five thousand mounted men raced at one another at a full gallop. Neither side slowed its charge; neither side veered away. They collided at a combined speed of fifty miles per hour "with a sound like the falling of timber." Horses and men crashed into one another with such force that horses were turned end over end, throwing their riders and crushing them beneath their own tangled bodies. Gregg had posted Captain William Miller's squad of the 3rd Pennsylvania in a line of woods along Low Dutch Road (5) with orders to hold his position. But Miller saw at once that he had an opportunity to strike the enemy on the flank. He charged into the rebel left just as two other squads assailed the right (6). Having failed to carry the field by a coup de main, and under attack from three sides, the Confederates withdrew to their original position.

Dramatic as it was, the cavalry action east of Gettysburg had no impact on the outcome of the battle. Custer later claimed that his charge had prevented Stuart from attacking Cemetery Ridge from the rear; Stuart denied it, asserting that since his assignment had been to protect the rebel left, he was the victor. In fact, there were no victors.

RETREAT
AND
PURSUIT
July 5 - July 12, 1863

At Meade's headquarters less than a quarter mile behind the battle front on Cemetery Hill, the Union commander was at the center of the maelstrom, but frustrated by the lack of clear information about the course of events. Reports from the front were spotty and infrequent as officers devoted themselves to the business at hand. At the crisis moment around 4:00 p.m., as the sound of the fighting on Cemetery Ridge rose to a crescendo, he quit his headquarters and, accompanied only by his son who was serving as a courier, he rode toward the battlefront to see for himself. In the furious and confused melee atop Cemetery Ridge, where a thousand men fought amidst the thick white smoke of a thousand rifles and scores of artillery pieces, Meade could not immediately grasp the progress of events.

"Have they turned?" Meade shouted at a nearby officer. "Yes, sir," the officer replied, pointing. "They are just turning." Then he saw it: hundreds, thousands, of men, individually and in small groups, were streaming back

Meade watches the repulse of Pickett's Charge from atop Cemetery Ridge. (National Archives)

across the open fields to Seminary Ridge. Near at hand, a group of Confederate prisoners, ordered to the rear by their captors, approached him. Recognizing an officer by his shoulder straps, they asked Meade where they should go. Meade pointed them to the rear, and they plodded on disconsolately, virtually unescorted. In front of the lines, the Union troops who had withstood the charge clambered up onto the stone wall, or climbed over it into the fields beyond to watch the retreat and gather souvenirs from the battlefield. Relief and euphoria struggled with exaltation. Someone raised a cheer and it spread along the line in both directions. Men waved their hats over their heads; in front of the line a Union officer on horseback raced back and forth with a captured Confederate flag tied to his saddle. Meade spoke quietly to himself: "Thank God."

Across the fields atop Seminary Ridge, Lee watched the remnants of his army stream back toward him, the men moving independently, hardly looking back. Knowing that they would be demoralized, and half expecting that Meade would follow up his advantage by launching a

The Taneytown Road and Meade's headquarters in a photo taken the day after the battle. (Library of Congress)

counter-attack, Lee spurred Traveller forward and rode out into the fields to meet them. "Never mind," he told them, "the fault is all mine. . . . I thought my men were invincible." Lee's emotions, too, were conflicted. He felt the burden of the defeat, and the loss of all those young lives. When Brigadier General John Imboden rode to Lee's headquarters late that evening, he was shocked to find Lee so thoroughly exhausted that he was barely able to dismount or even to stand unassisted. But then, Imboden wrote later, "he suddenly straightened up to his full height, and . . . said in a voice tremulous with emotion: 'I never saw troops behave more magnificently than Pickett's division of Virginians did today. . . .' " The moment did not last. As if recalling what had happened at the end of that gallant charge, Lee slumped again, and "in a tone almost of agony," he moaned, "Too bad! Oh, too bad."

The Confederate losses were horrible—even worse, if that were possible, than was immediately evident. When Lee told a downcast Pickett to form his division on the reverse slope of Seminary Ridge, Pickett responded sullenly, "General Lee, I have no division now." For all practical purposes, he was right. All three of Pickett's brigade commanders had fallen: Garnett was dead on the field, his body stripped of its badges of rank so that it was never identified; Armistead was mortally wounded and a prisoner; Kemper was so badly hurt he was not expected to survive the night. Out of the fifteen regimental commanders in the division, only one returned unscathed; of the 5,000 men of Pickett's division who made the charge, only 1,000 reported for duty the next morning.

Losses were heavy on the Union side of the field, too. Hancock, who had done more than anyone to win the day, was severely wounded just at the moment of his triumph when a ball penetrated his saddle horn and entered his groin driving a nail from the saddle into him as well. Though he was in terrible pain, he refused to let himself be carried from the field until he was sure that the enemy attack had failed. Gibbon, whose division manned the line along the stone wall by the clump of trees, was wounded as well. His division had lost 40 percent of its force killed and wounded; Webb's Brigade had lost 47 percent. One young officer, a captain in the 20th Maine, described the devastation in a letter to his wife:

"Heaven save you from the distress of such scenes—blackened and mangled corpses— dead horses— guns and equipment broken and strewn—trees cut and mangled—fences demolished—the grounds trodden, muddy and messy—and an almost intolerable stench— confusion all about—burying dead—hauling away wounded etc. etc. Oh, what scenes!"

Despite the losses, it was not as clear to the participants at the time as it is now looking back on it, that the battle was over. Meade thought Lee might try again; Lee expected Meade to counterattack. Indeed, before he had

The Federal army marches southward in the rain in pursuit of Lee's retreating column in this painting by Edwin Forbes. (Library of Congress)

Federal cavalry—in this case the 6th Michigan—tests the strength of Confederate defenses around Williamsport. Despite an effective pursuit, Meade let his corps commanders convince him that an all-out assault on Lee's position would be suicidal, and on July 14 Lee escaped into Virginia. (Library of Congress)

allowed himself to be carried from the field, Hancock had offered Meade a plan for a counterattack. But Meade was not eager to test the fates, and he had just witnessed the results of an attack across those open fields. He rode to Cemetery Hill to visit Howard and then headed south along the whole line of Cemetery Ridge to Little Round Top to inspect the lines and encourage the troops. As he passed, the soldiers stood and cheered him. One staff officer suggested that he was in great danger of becoming the next president.

For his part, Lee ordered his men to the reverse slope of Seminary Ridge where he had them prepare a line of entrenchments, beyond the view of the Federals, from which his battered army could repel the anticipated Federal attack. If Meade had tried to finish Lee off, he would have found it no easy matter.

But there was no Federal attack. The next morning both armies remained in place as if each side were waiting for the other to commit itself. Though he put up a bold front, Lee had already made the decision to retreat. The wagons, escorted by a single brigade of cavalry, would start as early as possible on the fourth. The infantry would depart that night. Meanwhile, both sides waited and watched each other across the open fields. As they watched, a hard, driving summer rain began to fall, provoking some to wonder if the very heavens were not determined to cleanse the fields of the blood that had been shed there.

That night, Lee started his infantry on the first leg of the long homeward journey. Meade did not hinder him. Not until the next day, July 5, did the Union commander send forward a reconnaissance in force to determine the disposition and strength of the enemy line. Once it was evident that Lee's army had decamped, Meade set out in pursuit. He had already sent his cavalry under Pleasanton, now he set the infantry in motion as well. But his pursuit would be cautious. Wounded as it was, the Confederate army was still a dangerous instrument of war, capable of turning on its pursuer.

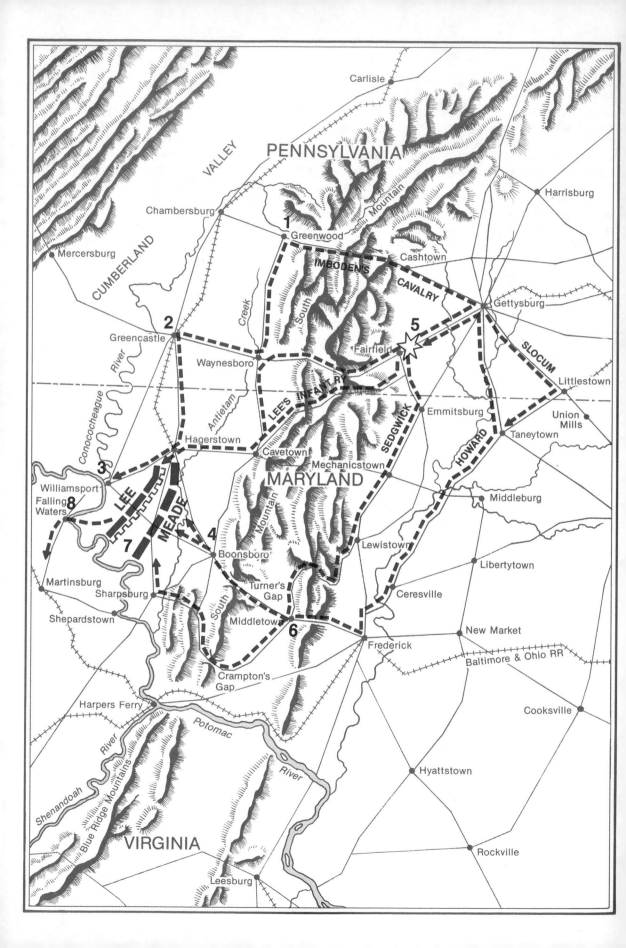

MAP 23

March to the Potomac

July 5 - July 14, 1863

Even before the sun set on July 3, it was evident to Lee that he had little option but to retreat the way he had come: westward through the passes of South Mountain, and then south through Maryland to friendly Virginia. That night he ordered Brigadier General John Imboden to escort the army's wagon train back to Virginia. Imboden started at 5:30 p.m. the next day. Not all the wounded could be carried off in the wagons—6,800 of them had to be left behind, partly because it was almost certain that the trip would kill them. Even as it was, many of the wounded found the tortuous bumping and rocking of the wagons so hellish that they cried out for someone to kill them, or to let them off by the side of the road so that death could take them quietly. All night, as the wagons rolled through the rain, wounded Confederate soldiers cried out, "O, God! Why can't I die?"

This goulish caravan—seventeen miles long—took the Cashtown Road as far as Greenwood (1), then turned south on a secondary road through Waynesboro to Greencastle (2) where it arrived on the morning of July 5. At Greencastle, the wagon train encounted its first opposition and from an unlikely source. Seeing their enemy in retreat, the citizens of the town were emboldened to attack the wagons, chopping the spokes out of wheels and rendering several of the wagons useless. Worse yet, Union cavalry patrols began to harry the train. Imboden's troopers had to conduct a fighting retreat all the way to Williamsport on the Potomac (3) where they arrived on the afternoon of July 5.

The Potomac offered no escape. The heavy rains had raised the level of the river so that it was too deep to ford. Imboden used two small rafts to ferry the walking wounded across, but those who could not walk, plus the wagons and the horses, were stuck on the northern bank. Late in the afternoon John Buford's brigade of Union cavalry advanced on Imboden's position at Williamsport along the road from Boonsboro (4). Imboden armed his wagon drivers and put up a bold front, firing his artillery as fast as the guns could be served and managed to hold off Buford's force until Stuart arrived with reinforcements.

As the Confederate wagon train was rolling out the Cashtown Road, the Confederate infantry was preparing to decamp as well. For them, too, the goal was to get behind the protecting shield of South Mountain. Well past dark on July 4, the soldiers of Lee's army quit Seminary Ridge and headed west out the Fairfield Road. Hill's Corps led, followed by Longstreet, with Ewell's Corps as the rear guard.

In early morning hours of July 5, Sedgwick's reconnaissance in force encountered the Confederate rear guard near Fairfield (5), specifically, he ran into John B. Gordon's Brigade. Gordon conducted a fighting retreat through the town and convinced Sedgwick that Lee intended to hold the passes through South Mountain. Meade wanted Sedgwick to press the issue, for he had two more corps within supporting distance and he was anxious to catch Lee and defeat him if he could. Sedgwick was less eager. He reported that it was foolish to attack Lee's army in the narrow defiles of South Mountain, in terrain so well suited to the defense. Reluctantly, Meade gave up the idea of a direct pursuit and determined to move southward on the eastern side of South Mountain, then cross through the passes at Turner's Gap and Crampton's Gap west of Middletown, Maryland (6).

The First, Third and Sixth Corps, all under Sedgwick's command, took the most direct route southwest through Emmitsburg, Mechanicstown (now Thurmont), and Lewistown; the Fifth and Eleventh Corps, both under Howard, marched due south to Taneytown, and then on to Frederick before turning west; and the Second and Twelfth Corps, under Slocum, marched southeast to Littlestown before angling southwest through Taneytown to follow Howard to Frederick. The Union soldiers performed marches that would have impressed Stonewall Jackson's "foot cavalry," some of them covering well over thirty miles before arriving at the rendezvous late on the evening of July 7. It took most of July 8 to cross the mountains, and by July 9, the Union army was only a few miles east of Williamsport (7).

Meanwhile, Lee's infantry had joined Imboden and his wagon train at Williamsport to find the river impassable. He put his men to work preparing entrenchments to defend his enclave while his engineers assembled a pontoon bridge across the river at Falling Waters (8). By the time Meade had his army reorganized and ready to advance, the Confederate entrenchments were formidable. At a meeting of Meade's corps commanders on July 12, most expressed the opinion that an attack against such a position was a bad idea, and Meade bowed to their views. Two days later he conducted a reconnaisance in force of the Confederate position. By then Lee was gone. His infantry had crossed on the pontoon bridges on the night of July 13 and the next day his infantry was back in the relative safety of Virginia. The campaign was over.

EPILOGUE
The Confederacy at Ebb Tide

On the very day that Lee flung the flower of his army against the center of the Union line near the clump of trees, another encounter between Union and Confederate commanders was taking place on a small knoll outside Vicksburg, Mississippi. Having endured a siege of 46 days, Confederate General John C. Pemberton met with Union commander Ulysses S. Grant to discuss terms of surrender. Grant offered no terms other than "unconditional surrender," and Pemberton responded, "Then, sir, it is unnecessary that you and I should hold any further conversation." But Pemberton had no other realistic alternative. Grant suggested that their staffs get together to discuss possible arrangements and the two army commanders stepped aside for a long period of quiet and rather strained conversation while their staffs worked out the details. When they rejoined the staff officers, a deal had been struck. It was not unconditional surrender, but nearly so. The Confederate army would march out of Vicksburg and stack arms. The men would be given their parole—a pledge not to fight again unless duly exchanged—and Grant's army would enter and

Ulysses S. Grant and John C. Pemberton discuss terms of surrender between the opposing lines at Vicksburg on July 3, the same day as Pickett's Charge. As a result of their discussion, the Confederates surrendered both Vicksburg and its defending army the next day. (M. and M. Karolik Collection, Museum of Fine Arts, Boston)

occupy Vicksburg. On July 4, thirty thousand Confederate soldiers were removed from the strategic chessboard, and with the fall of Port Hudson five days later, the Confederacy was torn asunder. As Lincoln expressed it so eloquently, the father of waters once more flowed unvexed to the sea.

The news from Vicksburg and the news from Gettysburg arrived in Richmond simultaneously. The twin blows of Lee's defeat and the loss of the Mississippi River were devastating to Confederate hopes and seemed to foreshadow ultimate defeat, still a year and ten months away. Chief of Ordnance Josiah Gorgas wrote in his diary that night that "Yesterday we rode the pinnacle of success, today absolute ruin seems to be our portion." President Jefferson Davis, generally unflaggingly optimistic, agreed. "We are now in the darkest hour of our political existence," he wrote.

Of course it was still possible to hope. Britain or France might come into the war on the Confederate side to salvage victory; the northern population might tire of the war, and its cost, and force the Lincoln administration to sue for peace; Lincoln might fail to be reelected in 1864. But what seemed increasingly unlikely after Gettysburg and Vicksburg was that the Confederacy could win its independence by force of arms. There would be other Confederate victories—at Chickamauga, Spotsylvania, and Kennesaw Mountain—but from the high water mark at Cemetery Ridge, the tide ebbed almost steadily through the bitter

Lincoln delivers his brief but eloquent address at the dedication of the National Cemetery at Gettysburg in November 1863. Lincoln is not visible without a magnifying glass in this photo; he stands bareheaded in the group of dignitaries at left center. (National Archives)

winter of 1864-65 and on to Appomattox.

Because of that, armchair strategists have often speculated about what might have happened had the Confederacy won the Battle of Gettysburg—if Ewell had seized Cemetery Hill on the evening of July 1; if Longstreet had rolled up the Union flank on July 2; if Pickett and Pettigrew had smashed through the center of the Union line on July 3. It is an intriguing speculation, and more than a few have suggested that with a Confederate victory at Gettysburg, the Confederacy might have won the war. But it is unlikely. Lee would have held Gettysburg, perhaps Stuart would have pursued the defeated Union army. But Meade's soldiers were veterans, and even in defeat they would not have been scattered by the 5,000 or so mounted troopers that Stuart had available. Sooner or later, and most likely sooner, Meade would have made another stand and Lee would have had to decide whether to attack again. Even in victory, Lee would have found himself in south-central Pennsylvania with an army of 50,000 men, burdened by 15,000 wounded, and with only enough ammunition for one more day's fighting. In the end, he would have had to retreat anyway.

In November, four months after the battle and with the war having moved back to Virginia, Abraham Lincoln traveled to Gettysburg to participate in the dedication ceremonies for the national cemetery that would adjoin the one already located on Cemetery Hill. He was preceded to the outdoor podium by Edward Everett of Massachusetts, a well-known and much-honored public speaker. Everett spoke for more than two hours and with powerful eloquence. When Lincoln rose to speak bareheaded on that chilly afternoon, the crowd was still resettling itself.

The president spoke from a prepared text, bending over a piece of paper that he held in his hand as it fluttered in the chill wind. Those furthest away did not hear his speech at all, and many who were nearby remembered only part of it. Everett was complimentary afterward, telling Lincoln that he had expressed the issue more clearly in two minutes than Everett himself had been able to do in two hours. Most, however, could not recall his remarks with any detail. It was only later, when the address was printed in the newspapers that it caught the attention of the public, for it did indeed capture clearly and powerfully the meaning not only of the day, and of the battle that was being commemorated, but of the whole war.

Gettysburg Address

Four score and seven years ago our fathers brought forth, on this continent, a new nation, conceived in Liberty, and dedicated to the proposition that all men are created equal.

Now we are engaged in a great civil war, testing whether that nation, or any nation so conceived, and so dedicated, can long endure. We are met on a great battlefield of that war. We have come to dedicate a portion of that field, as a final resting place for those who here gave their lives, that that nation might live. It is altogether fitting and proper that we should do this.

But, in a larger sense, we can not dedicate—we can not consecrate—we can not hallow—this ground. The brave men, living and dead, who struggled here, have consecrated it far above our poor power to add or detract. The world will little note, nor long remember what we say here, but it can never forget what they did here. It is for us the living, rather, to be dedicated here to the unfinished work which they who fought here have thus far so nobly advanced. It is rather for us to be here dedicated to the great task remaining before us—that from these honored dead we take increased devotion to that cause for which they here gave the last full measure of devotion—that we here highly resolve that these dead shall not have died in vain—that this nation, under God, shall have a new birth of freedom—and that government of the people, by the people, for the people, shall not perish from the earth.

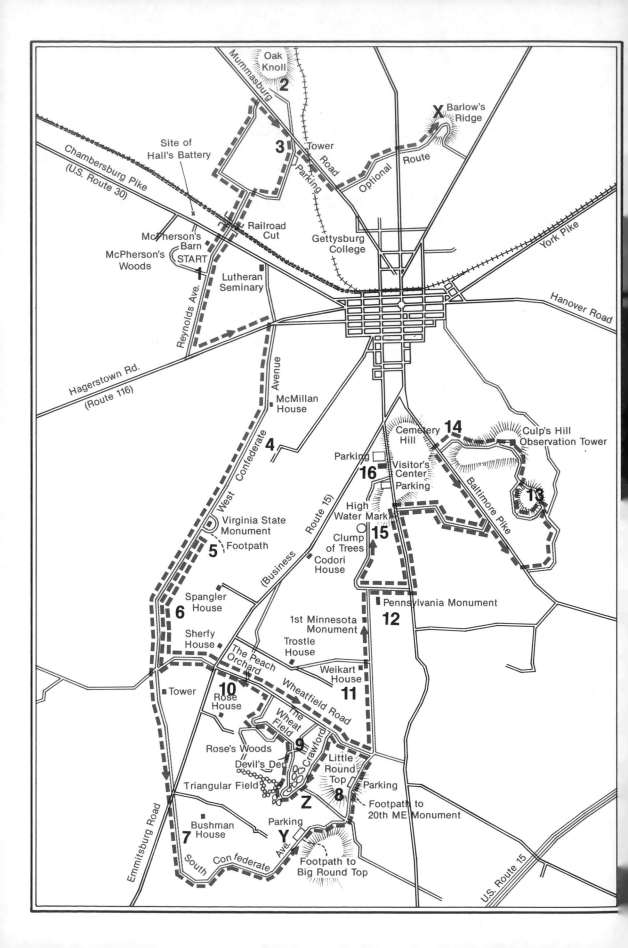

MAP 24

The Battlefield Today

The map at left shows Gettysburg and its roads as they existed in 1863. The roads shown in gray were built since the battle, including the auto tour route of the National Park Service. To follow the events of the battle in more-or-less chronological sequence by car requires some backtracking, and the route suggested here (marked in blue) deviates from the National Park Service tour only in a few details. Begin your tour on Reynolds Avenue along the crest of McPherson's Ridge between the Hagerstown Road and the Chambersburg Pike (1). The numbers on the map correspond with the stop numbers of the National Park Service tour. The table below correlates those numbers with the battle maps in this book.

The tour stop number appears first in each section below, followed by the pertinent map numbers.

1 6-7 McPHERSON'S RIDGE: Park just south of the Chambersburg Pike at the site where General Reynolds was killed. The woods to your left (west) are McPherson's Woods. Walk north, crossing the Chambersburg Pike (be careful, there are no crosswalks), and peer into the railroad cut. There are tracks in the cut today, but in 1863 it was only a dusty bed. Along the cut to your right you can find the small square stones showing where the 6th Wisconsin regiment crossed the cut to take the Confederates in a crossfire. A hundred yards west, out the Chambersburg Pike near the equestrian statue of Reynolds, is the site of Hall's Battery.

(Follow the auto tour northward but by-pass the Peace Monument (2) by turning right on the Mummasburg Road. Drive 1/4 mile on this road, and turn right into the parking area by the metal observation tower.)

3 8 THE HINGE: Climb the observation tower at the hinge of the Federal line between Wadsworth's Division and Robinson's Division. From here it is easy to see how the Federals faced attacks from both the west and the north at the same time. Note, too, the lack of cover for the soldiers of Howard's Corps north of town.

(If you choose, you may return to the Mummasburg Road and drive another 1/4 mile toward town, turning left onto a side road out to Barlow's Knoll (X), which is not on the Park Auto Tour. Here Francis Barlow fell wounded and the Federals broke. Afterward, return to the tower and follow the Auto Tour route south back to Reynolds Avenue. By-pass stops 4, 5, and 6, and go to stop 7 just across the Emmitsburg Road.)

7 10-11 BIESECKER'S WOODS: Hood's Division formed up in the shade of Biesecker's Woods on the afternoon of July 2. To your front is the stone and brick Bushman House. Beyond it, on a direct line, is the rocky summit of Little Round Top. Big Round Top is just to the right. The thickness of the woods to your front suggests the difficulty of maintaining a coordinated assault across a broad front in such terrain.

(Continue along the tour route to the parking lot at Big Round Top—there is no Auto Tour stop number here.)

Y 13 BIG ROUND TOP: There is a foot path up the steep slope of Big Round Top. As you climb, you can imagine the fatigue of Oates' Alabamians who ascended this hill on a hot July day before attacking Little Round Top. The monument to the 20th Maine on top shows that unit's position on July 3.

8 13 LITTLE ROUND TOP: Here you have an excellent view of Devil's Den and the valley of Plum Run ("The Slaughter Pen") to the west, and of Cemetery Ridge to the north. In addition be sure to cross the road and walk the trail out to the 20th Maine monument on Vincent's Spur. This marked the extreme left of the Federal line on July 2 and was the scene of Chamberlain's unexpected counterattack.

(Just beyond Little Round Top, turn left onto the Wheatfield Road, then left again onto Crawford Avenue. It is easy to miss—look for the cattle guard crossing.)

Z 12 DEVIL'S DEN: The triangular mountain meadow that was the center of much of the fighting for Devil's Den is on the western face beyond the impressive boulders.

9 14 WHEAT FIELD: Three tenths of a mile past the high point of Devil's Den, you enter the Wheat Field. The stone wall on your left is the one used by

De Trobriand; the heavy woods beyond are Rose's Woods, the original position of Barnes' Division. As you proceed, note the many monuments to Caldwell's Division which came crashing into the melee.

(Past "The Loop," turn left onto the Wheatfield Road and continue on to the Peach Orchard. NOTE: Do not turn right to follow the Auto Tour, but continue on to the Emmitsburg Road.)

10 15 PEACH ORCHARD: Note the Federal batteries pointing south along the Wheat Field Road—these were the guns that tore into Kershaw's Brigade as it advanced. But note, too, the sharp angle at the Peach Orchard where Sickles' line bent northward to follow the Emmitsburg Road, subjecting Graham's Brigade to attacks from two sides.

(Cross the Emmitsburg Road and return to West Confederate Avenue, turning right to return to the Virginia Monument at Auto Tour stop #5.)

5 16, 19-20 SEMINARY RIDGE: The Virginia State monument, with its impressive equestrian statue of Lee, marks the spot from which Wright's Brigade assailed the Union line late in the afternoon on July 2, and from which Lee observed Pickett's Charge on July 3. As you look across the field, the umbrella-shaped clump of trees on Cemetery Ridge is still clearly visible. Pettigrew, with Trimble behind him, formed in the woods on your left; Pickett formed in the woods on your right. Walk the footpath out to the fields where Lee met the survivors of Pickett's Charge.

(Retrace your route back across the Emmitsburg Road and along the Wheatfield Road, turning left onto Sedgwick Avenue.)

12 16 CEMETERY RIDGE: Near the gigantic Pennsylvania Monument, be sure to stop and read the inscription on the monument to the 1st Minnesota.

(Near the Pennsylvania Monument, the Park Auto Tour takes you to Culp's Hill via Meade's headquarters. The challenging terrain and heavy forestation of Culp's Hill helps explain the difficulty each side had in coordinating attacks, especially in the evening dusk of July 2 and the pre-dawn darkness of July 3. If you are pressed for time, you can by-pass Culp's Hill and continue on to the Angle. Otherwise, after you re-trace your route back to the Pennsylvania Monument, proceed to the Angle.)

15 21 THE ANGLE: At the Angle, note the stone tablet marking the spot where Armistead fell (the engraving has faded and is hard to read now, it is the tablet shaped like a scroll). More recently, advocates of North Carolina's claim to achieving the true "High Tide" of the Confederacy placed a marble monument a few dozen yards to the north beyond the stone wall. Small tablets along the stone wall show the location not only of each regiment, but each company.

Before you leave Gettysburg, be sure to stop at the Visitor's Center (16), and the National Cemetery across the street where Abraham Lincoln delivered his famous address in November, 1863.

———————

APPENDIX A
ORDER OF BATTLE

THE ARMY OF THE POTOMAC

Major General George Gordon Meade, Commander

I. **First Army Corps,**
Maj. Gen. John F. REYNOLDS
(Maj. Gen. Abner DOUBLEDAY)
(Maj. Gen. John NEWTON)

First Division:
Maj. Gen. James S. WADSWORTH
  First ("Iron") Brigade:
  Brig. Gen. Solomon MEREDITH
  (Col. William W. ROBINSON)
  Second Brigade:
  Brig. Gen. Lysander CUTLER

Second Division:
Brig. Gen. John C. ROBINSON
  First Brigade:
  Brig. Gen. Gabriel PAUL
  (Col. Samuel H. LEONARD)
  (Col. Adrian R. ROOT)
  (Col. Richard COULTER)
  (Col. Peter LYLE)
  Second Brigade:
  Brig. Gen. Henry BAXTER

Third Division:
Brig. Gen. Thomas A. ROWLEY
(Maj. Gen. Abner DOUBLEDAY)
  First Brigade:
  Col. Chapman BIDDLE
  (Brig. Gen. Thomas A. ROWLEY)
  Second Brigade: Col. Roy STONE
  (Col. Langhorne WISTER)

  (Col. Edmund L. DANA)
  Third Brigade:
  Brig. Gen. George STANNARD
  (Col. Francis V. RANDALL)

Artillery:
Col. Charles S. WAINWRIGHT

II. **Second Army Corps,**
Maj. Gen. Winfield Scott HANCOCK
(Brig. Gen. John GIBBON)

First Division:
Brig. Gen. John C. CALDWELL
  First Brigade:
  Col. Edward E. CROSS
  (Col. H. Boyd McKEEN)
  Second ("Irish") Brigade:
  Col. Patick KELLY
  Third Brigade:
  Brig. Gen. Samuel ZOOK
  (Lt. Col. John FRAZER)
  Fourth Brigade:
  Col. John R. BROOKE

Second Division:
Brig. Gen. John GIBBON
(Brig. Gen. William HARROW)
  First Brigade:
  Brig. Gen. William HARROW
  (Col. Francis E. HEATH)
  Second ("Philadelphia") Brigade:
  Brig. Gen. Alexander WEBB

Third Brigade:
Col. Norman J. HALL

Third Division:
Brig. Gen. Alexander HAYS
First Brigade:
Col. Samuel S. CARROLL
Second Brigade:
Col. Thomas A. SMYTHE
(Lt. Col. Francis E. PIERCE)
Third Brigade:
Col. George L. WILLARD
(Col. Eliakim SHERRILL)
(Lt. Col. James M. BULL)

Artillery:
Capt. John G. HAZARD

III.   **Third Army Corps,**
Maj. Gen. Daniel E. SICKLES
(Maj. Gen. David B. BIRNEY)

First Division:
Maj. Gen. David B. BIRNEY
(Brig. Gen. J. H. Hobart WARD)
First Brigade:
Brig. Gen. Charles GRAHAM
(Col. Andrew H. TIPPIN)
Second Brigade:
Brig. Gen. J. H. Hobart WARD
(Col. Hiram BERDAN)
Third Brigade:
Col. P. Regis De TROBRIAND

Second Division:
Brig. Gen. Andrew A. HUMPHREYS
First Brigade:
Brig. Gen. Joseph CARR
Second Brigade:
Col. William BREWSTER
Third Brigade:
Col. George C. BURLING

Artillery:
Capt. George E. RANDOLPH
(Capt. A. Judson CLARK)

V.   **Fifth Army Corps,**
Maj. Gen. George SYKES

First Division:
Brig. Gen. James BARNES
First Brigade:
Col. William S. TILTON
Second Brigade:
Col. Jacob B. SWEITZER
Third Brigade:
Col. Strong VINCENT
(Col. James C. RICE)

Second Division:
Brig. Gen. Romeyn AYRES
First Brigade:
Col. Hannibal DAY
Second Brigade:
Col. Sidney BURBANK
Third Brigade:
Col. Stepehn H. WEED
(Col. Kenner GERRARD)

Third Division:
Brig. Gen. Samuel W. CRAWFORD
First Brigade:
Col. William McCANDLESS
Third Brigade:
Col. Joseph FISHER

Artillery:
Capt. Augustus P. MARTIN

VI.   **Sixth Army Corps,**
Maj. Gen. John SEDGWICK

First Division:
Brig. Gen. Horatio G. WRIGHT
First Brigade:
Brig. Gen. A.T.A. TORBERT
Second Brigade:
Brig. Gen. Joseph J. BARTLETT
Third Brigade:
Brig. Gen. David A. RUSSELL

Second Division:
Brig. Gen. Albion P. HOWE
Second Brigade:
Col. Lewis A. GRANT
Third Brigade:
Brig. Gen. Thomas H. NEILL

Third Division:
Maj. Gen. John NEWTON
(Brig. Gen. Frank WHEATON)
  First Brigade:
  Brig. Gen. Alexander SHALER
  Second Brigade:
  Col. Henry L. EUSTIS
  Third Brigade:
  Brig. Gen. Frank WHEATON
  (Col. David J. NEVIN)

Artillery:
Col. Charles H. TOMPKINS

XI. Eleventh Army Corps,
  Maj. Gen. Oliver O. HOWARD
  (Maj. Gen. Carl SCHURZ)

First Division:
Brig. Gen. Francis C. BARLOW
(Brig. Gen. Adelbert AMES)
  First Brigade:
  Col. Leopold Von GILSA
  Second Brigade:
  Brig. Gen. Adelbert AMES
  (Col. Andrew L. HARRIS)

Second Division:
Brig. Gen. Adolph Von STEINWEHR
  First Brigade:
  Col. Charles R. COSTER
  Second Brigade:
  Col. Orlando SMITH

Third Division:
Maj. Gen. Carl SCHURZ
(Brig. Gen. Alexander
SCHIMMELFENNIG)
  First Brigade:
  Brig. Gen. Alexander
  SCHIMMELFENNIG
  (Col. George Von AMSBERG)
  Second Brigade:
  Col. W. KRZYZANOWSKI

Artillery:
Maj. Thomas W. OSBORN

XII. Twelfth Army Corps,
  Maj. Gen. Henry W. SLOCUM
  (Brig. Gen. Alpheus WILLIAMS)

First Division:
Brig. Gen. Alpheus S. WILLIAMS
(Brig. Gen. Thomas H. RUGER)
  First Brigade:
  Col. Archibald L. McDOUGALL
  Second Brigade:
  Brig. Gen. Henry LOCKWOOD
  Third Brigade:
  Brig. Gen. Thomas H. RUGER
  (Col. Silas COLGROVE)

Second Division:
Brig. Gen. John W. GEARY
  First Brigade:
  Col. Chalres CANDY
  Second Brigade:
  Brig. Gen. Thomas L. KANE
  (Col. George A. COBHAM)
  Third Brigade:
  Brig. Gen. George S. GREENE

Artillery:
Lt. Edward D. MUHLENBERG

Cavalry Corps,
Maj. Gen. Alfred PLEASANTON

First Division:
Brig. Gen. John BUFORD
  First Brigade:
  Col. William GAMBLE
  Second Brigade:
  Col. Thomas C. DEVIN
  Reserve Brigade:
  Brig. Gen. Wesley MERRITT

Second Division:
Brig. Gen. David McM. GREGG
  First Brigade:
  Col. John B. McINTOSH
  Third Brigade:
  Col. Irvin GREGG

Third Division:
Brig. Gen. Judson KILPATRICK
  First Brigade:
  Brig. Gen. Elon FARNSWORTH
  (Col. Nathaniel RICHMOND)
  Second Brigade:
  Brig. Gen. George A. CUSTER

Artillery Reserve:
Brig. Gen. Robert O. TYLER
(Capt. James M. ROBERTSON)

THE ARMY OF NORTHERN VIRGINIA

General Robert E. Lee, Commander

I. First Army Corps:
Lieut. Gen. James LONGSTREET

McLAWS's DIVISION:
Maj. Gen. Lafayette McLAWS
Kershaw's Brigade:
Brig. Gen. J. B. Kershaw
Semmes' Brigade:
Brig. Gen. Paul J. SEMMES
(Col. Goode BRYAN)
Barksdale's Brigade:
Brig. Gen. William BARKSDALE
(Col. B. G. HUMPHREYS)
Wofford's Brigade:
Brig. Gen. William T. WOFFORD
Artillery:
Col. H. C. CABELL

PICKETT's DIVISION:
Maj. Gen. George E. PICKETT
Garnett's Brigade:
Brig. Gen. Richard B. GARNETT
(Maj. C. S. PEYTON)
Kemper's Brigade:
Brig. Gen. James L. KEMPER
(Col. Joseph MAYO, Jr.)
Armistead's Brigade:
Brig. Gen. Lewis A. ARMISTEAD
(Col. W. R. AYLETT)
Artillery:
Maj. James DEARING

HOOD's DIVISION:
Maj. Gen. John B. HOOD
(Brig. Gen. Evander M. LAW
Law's Brigade:

Brig. Gen. Evander M. LAW
(Col. James L. SHEFFIELD)
Robertson's Brigade:
Brig. Gen. Jerome B. ROBERTSON
Anderson's Brigade:
Brig. Gen. George T. ANDERSON
(Lt. Col. William LUFFMAN)
Benning's Brigade:
Brig. Gen. Henry L. BENNING
Artillery:
Maj. M. W. HENRY

Artillery Reserve:
Col. J. B. WALTON

II. Second Army Corps:
Lieut. Gen. Richard S. EWELL

EARLY's DIVISION:
Maj. Gen. Jubal A. EARLY
Hay's Brigade:
Brig. Gen. Harry T. HAYS
Smith's Brigade:
Brig. Gen. William SMITH
Hoke's Brigade:
Col. Isaac AVERY
(Col. A. C. GODWIN)
Gordon's Brigade:
Brig. Gen. John B. GORDON
Artillery:
Col. H. P. JONES

JOHNSON's DIVISION:
Maj. Gen. Edward JOHNSON
Steuart's Brigade:
Brig. Gen. George H. STEUART

Nicholl'sBrigade:
Col. J. M. WILLIAMS
The Stonewall Brigade:
Brig. Gen. James A. WALKER
Jones' Brigade:
Brig. Gen. John M. JONES
(Lt. Col R. H. DUGAN)
Artillery:
Maj. J. W. LATMER
(Capt. C. I. RAINE)

RODES' DIVISION:
Maj. Gen. Robert E. RODES
Daniel's Brigade:
Brig. Gen. Junius DANIEL
Iverson's Brigade:
Brig. Gen. Alfred IVERSON
Doles' Brigade:
Brig. Gen. George DOLES
Ramseur's Brigade:
Brig. Gen. Stephen D. RAMSEUR
O'Neal's Brigade:
Col. E. A. O'NEAL
Artillery:
Lt. Col. Thomas H. CARTER

III. **Third Army Corps,**
Lieut. Gen. Ambrose P. HILL

ANDERSON's DIVISION:
Maj. Gen. Richard H. ANDERSON
Wilcox's Brigade:
Brig. Gen. Cadmus M. WILCOX
Wright's Brigade:
Brig. Gen. A. R. WRIGHT
Mahone's Brigade:
Brig. Gen. William MAHONE
Perry's Brigade:
Col. David LANG
Posey's Brigade:
Brig. Gen. Carnot POSEY
Artillery:
Maj. John LANE

HETH's DIVISION:
Maj. Gen. Henry HETH
(Maj. Gen. James J. PETTIGREW)
First Brigade:
Maj. Gen. James J. PETTIGREW
(Col J. K. MARSHALL)
Second Brigade:
Col. J. M. BROCKENBROUGH

Third Brigade:
Brig. Gen. James J. ARCHER
(Col. B. D. FRY)
(Lt. Col. S. G. SHEPARD)
Fourth Brigade:
Brig. Gen. Joseph R. DAVIS
Artillery:
Lt. Col. John J. GARNETT

PENDER's DIVISION:
Maj. Gen. William D. PENDER
First Brigade:
Col. Abner PERRIN
Second Brigade:
Brig. Gen. James H. LANE
(Col. C. M. AVERY)
Third Brigade:
Brig. Gen. Edward L. THOMAS
Fourth Brigade:
Brig. Gen. A. M. SCALES
(Lt. Col. G. T. GORDON)
(Col W. Lee J. LOWRANCE)
Artillery:
Maj. William T. POAGUE

Cavalry Division,
Maj. Gen. James E. B. STUART

Hampton's Brigade:
Brig. Gen. Wade HAMPTON
(Col. L. S. BAKER)
Robertson's Brigade:
Brig. Gen. Beverly ROBERTSON
Jones' Brigade:
Brig. Gen. William E. JONES
Fitz Lee's Brigade:
Brig. Gen. Fitzhugh LEE
Jenkins' Brigade:
Brig. Gen. A. G. JENKINS
(Col. M. J. FERGUSON)
W.H.F. Lee's Brigade:
Col. J. R. CHAMBLISS
Horse Artillery:
Maj. R. F. BECKHAM

Imboden's Command:
Brig. Gen. J. D. Imboden

Artillery Reserve:
Col. R. Lindsay WALKER

[95]

APPENDIX B

CASUALTY FIGURES

Though each side kept records of the number of killed, wounded, and missing at Gettysburg, the official accounts are not completely trustworthy, and Confederate figures in particular are almost certainly low. For one thing, in accordance with Lee's directive, the Confederacy did not record as "wounded" those individuals who were still capable of performing their duties, thus there may have been several thousand lightly wounded Confederate who are not represented. Also, the category of "missing or captured" includes both those whose bodies were unrecovered and those who were captured and therefore lost for the campaign, but it also includes many who were merely stragglers and who might be expected to rejoin the army eventually. The numbers in the following tables represent a reasonable estimate of the number of killed and wounded rounded off to the nearest 100. In addition, each side recorded just over 5,000 "missing" over the three days of the battle.

TABLE #1: Killed and Wounded Each Day:

	UNION	CONFED- ERATE	TOTAL
Day 1	5,400	5,600	11,000
Day 2	9,000	6,000	15,000
Day 3	3,300	4,700	8,000
Total	17,700	16,300	34,000
Missing	5,400	5,200	10,600
Totals	23,100	21,500	44,600

TABLE #2: Killed and Wounded by Unit:

	UNION FORCES				CONFEDERATE FORCES		
	KILLED	CAP'D	TOTAL		KILLED	CAP'D	TOTAL
First Corps (Reynolds)	3,900	2,200	6,100	First Corps (Longstreet)	5,200	2,300	7,500
Second Corps (Hancock)	4,000	400	4,400	Second Corps (Ewell)	5,600	1,300	6,900
Third Corps (Sickles)	3,600	600	4,200	Third Corps (A.P. Hill)	5,200	1,500	6,700
Fifth Corps (Sykes)	2,000	200	2,200	Cavalry Div. (Stuart)	200	100	300
Sixth Corps (Sedgwick)	200	000	200	Misc. (Staff, Support, etc.)	100	000	100
Eleventh Corps (Howard)	2,300	1,500	3,800	Total	16,300	5,200	21,500
Twelfth Corps (Slocum)	1,000	100	1,100				
Cavalry Corps (Pleasanton)	400	400	800				
Artillery	200	000	200				
Misc. Staff, Support, etc.	100	000	100				
Total	17,700	5,400	23,100				

Suggestions for Further Reading

Few events in history have been as well chronicled as the three day battle at Gettysburg. The following is not intended as a bibliography, though all of these volumes were consulted in the preparation of this work. Rather, it is intended as a guide to further reading by the interested reader.

By far the best single-volume work on Gettysburg is Edwin B. Coddington's *The Gettysburg Campaign: A Study in Command* (New York, 1968). It is a lengthy work (866 pages including notes and index), but it is comprehensive without being dry, and Coddington offers thoughtful judgements about the participants as well as an accurate account of the events. Two other readable narrative accounts are Glenn Tucker's *High Tide at Gettysburg* (Indianapolis, 1958; Dayton, 1983) and Edward J. Stackpole, *They Met at Gettysburg* (Harrisburg, 1956). Richard Wheeler's *Witness to Gettysburg* (New York, 1987) is a compilation of eyewitness accounts and memoirs arranged chronologically to provide the reader with a sense of being present. Jay Luvaas and Harold W. Nelson also rely on contemporary reports in their work, *The U.S. Army War College Guide to the Battle of Gettysburg* (Carlisle, 1986). One of the most moving and evocative accounts is the *The Killer Angels* (New York, 1974), which though faithful to the events, is a novel by virtue of Shaara's presentation of what each of the major characters may have been thinking. All of these works are available in paperback editions.

Biographies have been written of both army commanders, and most of the corps commanders, on both sides. These studies offer a valuable and unique perspective by allowing the reader to view the battle through the eyes of one of the major participants. The following are among the best:

UNION OFFICERS:

Freeman Cleaves, *Meade of Gettysburg* (Norman, OK, 1960).

Edward J. Nichols, *Toward Gettysburg: A Biography of General John F. Reynolds* (University Park, PA, 1958).

Glenn Tucker, *Hancock, The Superb* (Indianapolis, 1960).

W. A. Swanburg, *Sickles, The Incredible* (New York, 1956).

Willard Wallace, *Soul of the Lion, A Biography of General Joshua L. Chamberlain* (New York, 1960).

CONFEDERATE OFFICERS:

Douglas Southall Freeman, *R. E. Lee, A Biography,* 4 vols. (New York, 1935). For a contrasting view, see Thomas L. Connelly's, *The Marble Man: Robert E. Lee and His Image in American Society* (New York, 1977), and Alan Nolan, *Lee Considered: General Robert E. Lee and Civil War History* (Chapel Hill, 1991).

H. J. Eckenrode and Bryan Conrad, *James Longstreet: Lee's War Horse* (Chapel Hill, 1936, 1986).

James I. Robertson, Jr., *General A. P. Hill: The Story of a Confederate Warrior* (New York, 1987).

Emory Thomas, *Bold Dragoon: The Life of J. E. B. Stuart* (New York, 1985).

Of all the regimental histories, two are especially worth reading for the crucial role played by those regiments at Gettysburg. They are John J. Pullen's *The Twentieth Maine: A Volunteer Regiment in the Civil War* (New York, 1957; Dayton, 1991), and Lance J. Herdegen and William J. K. Beaudot, *In The Bloody Railroad Cut At Gettysburg* (Dayton, 1990), about the 6th Wisconsin.

Finally, careful scholars have produced detailed accounts of each day's events. The first day of the fight is chronicled by Warren Hassler, Jr. in *Crisis at the Crossroads: The First Day at Gettysburg* (University, Alabama, 1970). The second day is examined with great care by Harry W. Pfanz in *Gettysburg: The Second Day* (Chapel Hill, 1987). And the climactic third day is dramatically reported by George R. Stewart in *Pickett's Charge: A Microhistory of the Final Attack at Gettysburg, July 3, 1863* (Boston, 1959; Dayton, 1983), as well as by Alan M. Hollingsworth in *The Third Day at Gettysburg: Pickett's Charge* (New York, 1959).

INDEX

CRAIG LEE SYMONDS is a native of southern California, and a graduate of U.C.L.A. He earned his Masters and Ph. D. degrees at the University of Florida, and served four years in the United States Navy, during which time he was a member of the faculty of the U.S. Naval War College in Newport, Rhode Island. He is the author of six books on naval and military history, including battlefield atlases of both the American Revolution and the Civil War as well as the biography of Confederate General Joseph E. Johnston. Currently he is professor of history and department chairman at the United States Naval Academy in Annapolis, Maryland where he lives with his wife Marylou.